Translation Practice

Translation Practices Explained is a series of coursebooks designed to help self-learners and teachers of translation.

Each volume focuses on a specific type of translation, in most cases corresponding to actual courses available in translator-training institutions. Special volumes are devoted to professional areas where labour-market demands are growing: court interpreting, community interpreting, European-Union texts, multimedia translation, text revision, electronic tools, and software and website localization.

The authors are practising translators or translator trainers in the fields concerned. Although specialists, they explain their professional insights in a manner accessible to the wider learning public.

Designed to complement the *Translation Theories Explained* series, these books start from the recognition that professional translation practices require something more than elaborate abstraction or fixed methodologies. The coursebooks are located close to work on authentic texts, simulating but not replacing the teacher's hands-on role in class. Self-learners and teachers are encouraged to proceed inductively, solving problems as they arise from examples and case studies. The series thus offers a body of practical information that can orient and complement the learning process.

Each volume includes activities and exercises designed to help self-learners consolidate their knowledge and to encourage teachers to think creatively about their classes. Updated reading lists and website addresses will also help individual learners gain further insight into the realities of professional practice.

Anthony Pym
Series Editor

Electronic Tools for Translators

Frank Austermühl

St. Jerome Publishing
Manchester, UK & Northampton, MA

Published by
   St. Jerome Publishing
   2 Maple Road West, Brooklands
   Manchester, M23 9HH, United Kingdom
   Tel +44 161 973 9856
   Fax +44 161 905 3498
   stjerome@compuserve.com
   http://www.stjerome.co.uk

ISBN 1-900650-34-7 (pbk)
ISSN 1470-966X (*Translation Practices Explained*)

Printed and bound in Great Britain by
T. J. International Ltd., Cornwall, UK

Cover design by
Steve Fieldhouse, Oldham, UK (+44 161 620 2263)

Typeset by
Delta Typesetters, Cairo, Egypt
Email: delttyp@starnet.com.eg

British Library Cataloguing in Publication Data
A catalogue record of this book is available from the British Library

Library of Congress Catalging-in-Publication Data
Austermühl, Frank.
   Electronic tools for translators / Frank Austermühl.
      p. cm. -- (Translation practices explained, ISSN 1470-966X)
   Includes bibliographical references and index.
   ISBN 1-900650-34-7 (Pbk. : alk. paper)
   1. Translating and interpreting--Data processing. I. Title. II.
Series.
   P308 .A88 2001
   418'.02'0285--dc21
                          2001000657

Contents

How to use this book

This book is addressed to translation trainers, students and professionals interested in the manifold possibilities offered by electronic tools for translators. It can also be used as a textbook for regular classes on computer-assisted translation or for translation practice classes, as well as for self-learning. Each chapter (with the exception of the chapters on the Internet) deals with a different tool and can be approached as an individual lesson.

The chapters are all structured in terms of five basic parts:

- A description of the general context of the subject to be dealt with, including the goals of the chapter and the resources and tools to be explained.
- An introduction to the nature of the tools discussed, including their position in the translation process, their operative principles and typical features, and criteria for their evaluation.
- Case studies showing the actual use of the tools discussed, including general strategies for things such as searching the Internet, browsing electronic dictionaries, or using online dictionaries.
- Tasks to be performed by students, intended to highlight the most important aspects of the chapters, to deepen understanding of the tools described in the chapter, and to motivate readers to integrate the tools into their daily training or work.
- Bibliography and links that provide information on further reading and information.

At the end of the book there is a general bibliography and lists of the Internet addresses and the products mentioned, along with an extensive index.

Although it is recommended that the reader work through the book in the order of presentation, individual access to selected topics is also possible. When you use the table of contents or the index provided, the book can easily become a reference work.

Although a number of tools are described in great detail, this book clearly does not claim to cover each and every single product available on the market. However, the most relevant types of tools are presented, and examples of each type are given. The focus is on general strategies, explained through numerous examples relevant to translation. Readers are invited to develop these strategies in terms of their own experience as translators. The tasks will hopefully deepen your understanding of the subject matter and arouse your appetite for more.

FA   Germersheim, Dec. 20, 2000
AP   Tarragona, Dec. 21, 2000

1. Translation in the information age

Perhaps more than other professionals, translators are feeling the long-term changes brought about by the information age. The snowballing acceleration of available information, the increase in intercultural encounters, and the continuing virtualization of private and business life have resulted in drastic and lasting changes in the way translators work.

The main task of translation – the transfer of technical and cultural information – can now only be achieved through the use of extensive knowledge bases. As a knowledge-based activity, translation requires new strategies and a paradigm shift in methodology. This shift must embrace practice, teaching and research.

The purpose of this book is to provide the reader with guidelines on how to incorporate electronic language resources into the translation process. This first chapter will describe the socio-economic background against which the use of computerized translation aids has to be seen. A new model for the integration and evaluation of electronic translation tools will then be introduced.

This chapter has the following general goals:

- to explain why translation, as a by-product of the information age and globalization, has become a computer-based activity;
- to describe the types of electronic tools available, the degrees to which they make the translation process automatic, and their functions within the translation process;
- to present a model of translation that can be used as a guide to the integration of electronic translation tools into translator training.

When reading this book, please bear in mind that the term 'electronic translation tools' does not refer exclusively to machine translation (MT). MT systems are only one of many kinds of translation tools. Indeed, since MT systems neglect the communicative, cultural and encyclopedic dimensions of translation, it is questionable whether they really provide 'translation' at all.

It is also important to understand that the tools demonstrated in this book are not replacements for human translation. There is no such thing as a computer-aided cure-all that will make a poor translator into a good one. However, used properly, the right tools can help good translators improve the efficiency and quality of their work. Indeed, quality is the primary yardstick for assessing electronic translation tools.

The need for electronic tools

Readers might ask themselves the following basic questions: First, as translators and cultural-linguistic mediators, do we need tools to assist us in our tasks?

And if so, do those tools need to be electronic? Instead of answering these questions immediately, I would like to set the stage by describing one of the contexts in which translation is currently being carried out. It is a context characterized by globalization, specialization and digitization.

Globalization

> Globalization: What happens when the degree of global human interaction increases to such an extent that both its primary effects and the reactions it provokes give rise to numerous new developments. General globalization is caused on three basic levels: technological globalization, political globalization and economic globalization. The three levels initiate a process in which geographical distance is diminished as a factor in the establishment and maintenance of border-crossing in long-distance economic, political and socio-cultural relations.(http://www.globalize.org/lexicon.asp?term=globalization)

The concept of globalization entails another crucial question, one that might make the entire translation profession obsolete: Do we, as citizens of the 'global village', really need translation at all? Why bother with 4,000 to 6,000 different languages if we can make do with only one, namely English? After all, English is the dominant language in international politics, business, technology, science, education, aviation, seafaring, etc. It is the *lingua franca* of the global market economy, especially in the field of business–to–business communication. For example, 80 percent of all business transactions in Denmark are carried out in English (Lockwood 1998:16). International business negotiations and contract talks among non-native English speakers from Algeria and Germany are conducted in English. The importance of English as a promoter of economic growth is further demonstrated by the fact that within the Organization for Economic Co-operation and Development (OECD), English-speaking countries receive three times as much foreign direct investment as those where English is not the official language (Mai & Wettach 1999:130). Globally, many large corporations have adopted English as their official language. About 85 percent of international organizations use English as their working language. In Europe, 99 percent of all international organizations have English as one of their official languages (Mai & Wettach 1999:130). The world of technology, too, is heavily influenced by English, or more accurately by its American variety. Roughly 80 percent of the contents of the 1 billion Internet pages on the web at the time of writing are in English. Almost 60 percent of all Internet users are native speakers of English. The lion's share of the 8,000 online databases currently available is taken by information in the English language. The global scientific community, as another example, is even more monolingual. About 90 percent of all scientific publications are written in English (ibid.:130). Some 98 percent of all German physicists publish their findings in English, while 83 percent of their colleagues in the field of chemistry do the same. Even in France, two-thirds of scientists use English to communicate research results to a global audience (Raeithel 1999:1). Publications in German or French make up less than 3 percent of the total global number of scientific publications (http://www. br-online.de/bildung/deutsch2000/05_publikationen.html). The majority of Nobel Prizes go to laureates who are citizens of countries where English is the official language, and English is the default language for international scientific conferences, no matter where they take place or what their specific topics are.

So is English ringing the death knell for the rest of the world's languages? Is 'linguicide' in sight? Will the vision of a monolingual world lead to the end of translation?

Well, for the moment at least, the answer is no. Most notably, the European Union stands as one of the few bastions against linguistic uniformity, granting each of its current 15 member states the privilege of using their state languages to conduct their official business within EU institutions. This institutionalized multilingualism is made possible by the work of about 4,000 in-house translators, interpreters and terminologists, and many more freelancers. Each additional official language increases the demand by 250 to 300 linguists (Stoll 1999:17). With 11 official languages and 110 possible language-pair combinations, it is not surprising that in 1997 2 billion euros were spent on translation (including interpretation and terminology work). This does not include the more than 200,000 pages channelled through the EC-Systran MT system each year (European Commission 1999:16). With a possible expansion of the EU by as many as 12 new members and the integration of anywhere between 6 to 10 new languages, the number of combinations would increase exponentially, resulting in 420 combinations for 21 languages. Nevertheless, most of the expansion talks with future EU candidates are being conducted in English. Perhaps the EU will not be the sole saviour of translation.

Beyond political institutions, economic reasons may well contribute to keeping translators in business. This is because knowledge of foreign languages is not as widespread as one might assume. Only 28 percent of German executives, for example, consider their English skills to be very good. Nor is insecurity in English usage limited to the business sector. According to a 1999 study, about one in four German university professors would refrain from attending a conference if English were the sole working language (Mai & Wettach 1999:132). The increasingly multilingual nature of the business world can be explained to a large extent by the simple and ancient trading axiom that clients will only buy in their own language. For sellers, this implies the need to speak the language of the customer and to adapt their conduct and products to the specific characteristics of the local market. The globalized economy means that businesses are trying to sell the same goods – from iMacs to Eastpacks to Big Macs – in every corner of the world. This requires traders to accommodate their marketing and selling strategies to local idiosyncrasies. Globalization thus automatically entails localization, as is expressed in the term *glocalization* and slogans such as 'Think globally, act locally'.

A powerful catalyst for translation has thus been created by the rapid internationalization of markets, particularly by the need to localize not only products but also the methods of designing, producing, marketing and distribution.

The growing demand for translation

The increase in cross-border communications, intensified international competition and stricter product-related regulations have led to the rapid growth of international demand for translation. The German translation market, for example, has been experiencing a steady 14 percent annual increase for several years. Currently, the total annual translation demand from German businesses amounts to 30 million pages (http://dsb.uni-leipzig.de/~xlatio/FALT.HTM).

In 1997, the EU-funded ASSIM study estimated the total turnover of the translation markets of 18 member states of the European Union and the European Economic Area (EEA) to be 3.75 billion euros, with software, audio-visual and multimedia translations constituting 20 percent of the total turnover. According to that study, the total number of in-house and external translators exceeds 100,000 (http://www.hltcentral.org/usr_docs/project-source/Assim/ Assim-EN.doc). The global translation market, encompassing human and machine translation as well as software and website localization, is expected to grow from over US$10.4 billion in 1999 to close to US$17.2 billion in 2003, according to a study by Allied Business Intelligence (http://www.the-infoshop.com/study/ab3365_ languagetranslation.html).

The mushrooming of the electronic market will have a huge effect on the translation industry. In particular, the growing demand for the translation of websites and other forms of multimedia texts (e.g. for DVD productions) will add to this development. By 2002, transactions over the Internet will be worth more than US$400 billion (Gantz 1998). The demand for software localization will further contribute to the expansion of the industry. It is estimated that between 1994 and 1997, translation services underwent a growth rate of 55 percent and now have growth rates of up to 20 percent. However, note that between 1994 and 1997 employment among translators only rose by 18 percent (ASSIM 1997).

This increase in demand results from the development of the Internet from an English-only medium to an international platform for communication and information. Non-English speakers are the fastest growing group of new Internet users, with a rapidly growing interest in non-English sites as the Net becomes genuinely multilingual. Websites in Spanish, Portuguese, German, Japanese, Chinese and Scandinavian languages are showing the strongest growth rates. It is estimated that although 57.4 percent of Internet users were based in English-speaking countries in 1999, this figure will drop to 43 percent by 2005. Growth rates in the number of Internet users in non-English-speaking countries are already much higher than in English-speaking countries. While the number of English-speaking Internet users is expected to rise by 60 percent over the next six years, the number of non-English-speaking users is expected to increase by 150 percent. At the same time, it is estimated that the total number of Internet users worldwide will increase from 171 million in 1999 to 345 million in 2005. This will lead to a growing number of multilingual sites and thus to a growing demand for website translation.

Part of this increase in translation demand will be absorbed by more sophisticated methods of machine-aided translation. Also, owing to international competition, translation pay-rates might be expected to stagnate or even decline in the future. Nevertheless, globalization is definitively promoting the demand for translations and translators. This is also confirmed by the increasing number of translation programmes in universities worldwide. In Europe alone, there are about 80,000 students in 150 institutions studying translation on the level of higher education (ASSIM 1997). For an updated list of translator training institutions, see Anthony Pym's page at http://www.fut.es/~apym/tti/tti.htm (see also (see also Snell-Hornby 1998 and Pym 1998).

Digitization, automation and their impact on the translation market

Automation: The application of machines to tasks once performed by human beings or, increasingly, to tasks that would otherwise be impossible. [...]. Automation has revolutionized those areas in which it has been introduced, and there is scarcely an aspect of modern life that has been unaffected by it. (Encyclopaedia Britannica CD 2000)	*Digitize*: Function: transitive verb Inflected Form(s): -tized; -tiz·ing Date: 1953 to convert (as data or an image) to digital form dig·i·ti·za·tion noun dig·i·tiz·er noun (Oxford English Dictionary)

In addition to the developments in international competition and the expansion of the Internet, a further reason for the growing automation of translation is the general digitization of the global economy. When looking at the future of translation, it is important to understand the changes that international business and communication processes are undergoing. These changes are heavily influenced by the use of modern means of information and communication technology. Computer and communications systems are the most important factors for these developments. The telecommunications, networking and computer industries have jointly transformed industrial society into the information society we know today. The creation of a global network infrastructure and the digitization of commercial goods have permanently altered the way international business is conducted.

A significant part of the growth of the international market is due to the advent of free Internet accounts, particularly in Europe. Products and services are being coded into sequences of 0s and 1s, of bits and bytes, enabling them to travel around the world in fractions of a second. Computers have become universal, not only in terms of geographic distribution but also with regard to their use. The PC has evolved into a multifunctional communications and information-processing device used in every realm of life. Global computer networks and the Internet make information available any time and any place. Information has become a decisive factor for economic success, equalling or even surpassing the importance of the classical resources of labour and capital. The computer is becoming a universal medium for communication and co-operation. Concepts such as tele-working, virtual teams or computer-based collaboration show that the computer's initial function as a number-cruncher and data processor has been surpassed by its co-ordinative and supportive role.

These effects have changed the profile of almost all professional occupations. Computer skills or computer literacy have become a *sine qua non* for success. In the future, very few jobs will be manageable without the use of computers.

The influence of specialization and diversification on the translator

The translation market is influenced not only by globalization and digitization but also – and probably more strongly – by the enormous degree of technical specialization and economic diversification taking place today. A few selected 'factoids' demonstrate the extraordinary scale of the information explosion currently taking place:

- the amount of knowledge to be processed within the next decade is larger than the amount of knowledge accumulated during the past 2500 years;
- 90 percent of all scientists who have ever lived are alive and working today;
- 165,000 scientific journals are currently being published;
- 20,000 new scientific papers are produced every day (Markl 1998);
- the amount of data that is circulating on the Internet on any given day is larger than all the information available throughout the nineteenth century (*Der Spiegel* 1996);

- according to an estimate by Germany's Siemens corporation, the combined vocabulary of technical and scientific disciplines amounted to 30 million words in 1991. The study predicted a doubling within five years (Schneider 1991).

These figures demonstrate the scope of the information explosion that is taking place. Even Leonardo da Vinci, who is sometimes said to have been the last person with truly global knowledge, would not stand a chance of grasping even a small percentage of the knowledge available today. The increase in information resembles a flood of data in which the human brain can no longer alone be a Noah's Ark of knowledge. The brain's natural capacities have to be supported by electronic tools in order to help avoid a potential synaptic collapse. That means that in addition to the natural knowledge bases, electronic knowledge bases have to be provided.

The impact of ICT on translation

For translators there is no longer any question of whether or not to use computers and networks. The use of information and communication technology (ICT) is a *fait accompli* in the lives of today's language professionals. The electronic handling of orders and the digitized delivery of language services are now taken for granted as standard client services. For example, the European Commission's Language Service requires its external freelance translators to use a rather sophisticated IT infrastructure. More than 50 percent of the translators interviewed for the 1997 ASSIM report were using electronic dictionaries, and about one-third of the translators were using translation memory systems.

The application of institutional pressure is not the only way translators will be convinced to make extensive use of modern ICT systems. Exposure to the right approaches in using electronic tools will lead to a bottom-up automation of the translator's workplace, enabling translators to increase significantly their professional translation service quality and efficiency. These two effects – the improvement of quality and increased productivity – will clearly strengthen the position of any freelance translator in a rapidly changing and increasingly competitive global language market (Wood 1998).

Trends toward globalization and international networking have resulted in organizational changes in enterprises worldwide. In the resulting virtual enterprises, outsourcing and workflow-management systems have impacted on the translation business so greatly that we can now talk about 'tele-translation'. This concept is based on the assumption that translators can communicate with clients across the globe; they can compete for orders regardless of their location. A sophisticated IT infrastructure thus becomes a significant competitive advantage in terms of client acquisition. Furthermore, quick access to relevant and reliable online and offline data has become a key issue in the retrieval of encyclopedic and linguistic information necessary for the tasks being performed (Austermühl forthcoming).

It is obvious that the growing demand for high-quality translations of technical texts is no longer manageable without the use of computer-based methods. The increase in efficiency needed to deal with this growing demand can only be achieved by the expanded use of modern forms of ICT.

Electronic resources offer several distinct advantages. For a start, much of the content of specialized print dictionaries are already out of date by the time the books reach the market. To understand the reason for this, just look at the speed with which domain knowledge is being produced in some innovative disciplines such as ICT, bio-technology or immunology, and then compare this process with the time it takes to put together and publish a print dictionary. Electronic dictionaries, on the other hand, can be published online or offline (i.e. on CD-ROM) without any delay and can easily be kept up to date over the Internet. Many publishing houses have changed their strategies with regard to publishing reference works in general and have turned to publishing their works on CD-ROM or even online. The powerful presence of the *Encyclopaedia Britannica* (http://www.britannica.com) on the Internet underlines this process. Many specialized encyclopedias or scientific journals that have long been valuable resources for translators are no longer published in print but are only delivered digitally. Many newspapers and magazines offer online access to their archives, thereby allowing a comprehensive search of all articles within seconds. Printed versions simply cannot compete.

At the same time, the exchange of texts and information between translators and their clients is taking place almost exclusively over electronic channels. The traditional 'snail mail' has been replaced by its electronic brethren. In all these areas, dramatic modifications are being made to the way the business of translation is conducted. The advantages of modern information and communication systems are introducing new criteria of speed, flexibility, timeliness and comprehensiveness.

Typologies of electronic translation tools

As in many associated areas, the market for language-resource products is skyrocketing. The spectrum of electronic translation tools covers a wide range of state-of-the-art computer applications. It ranges from spellcheckers to machine-translation systems, from word-processing software to terminological databases, from electronic encyclopedias to online dictionaries, from HTML editors to software-localization tools. An electronic newspaper archive can be a valuable translation resource, and a videoconferencing system can serve as a powerful communications tool. The same is true of graphic software, mailing lists, translation memories or e-zines – electronic magazines.

The variety of electronic translation tools can be as confusing as it is re-markable. There have been many proposals for categorizing them. Here we will introduce three possible models for categorization, along with some of the basic terminology used in the discussion of computer-assisted translation in general.

The first model was introduced by Alan Melby in the early 1980s and repre-sents a functional approach to categorizing electronic translation tools. The second model categorizes existing translation tools according to the degree of automation that they introduce to the translation process. The third model is the one we have adopted as the theoretical basis of this book: it represents a process-oriented approach to the use and evaluation of the electronic transla-tion tools.

Melby's translator workstation

Figure 1 shows the three levels of the translator's workstation proposed by Alan Melby in the early 1980s.

Level 1	Text Processing Telecommunications Software Terminology Management Systems Others (DTP, Converter)
Level 2	Text Analysis Automatic Dictionary Look-up Bilingual Text Retrieval Other (SGML)
Level 3	Machine Translation

Figure 1. Melby's translator workstation (Melby 1982)

Only level 1 elements of Melby's model had been used on a broad scale by the mid-1990s; tools at levels 2 and 3 had only been partially implemented. At the end of twentieth century, however, these products were widely used in the professional translation world. CD-ROM-based dictionaries, encyclopedias and terminology management systems are now standard equipment for most translators.

Translation memory systems are being used by all major translation agen-cies, translation departments, and many freelances as well. Universal data exchange formats, such as SGML (Standard Generalized Markup Language), are becoming increasingly important, and machine translation systems – even with their less-than-perfect outputs – have found their way onto translators' desktops everywhere. True, automated text analysis is currently less widely used among freelances and agencies, although it could ultimately play a major role in translation-oriented quality management. However, this should also change with the availability of more efficient terminology extraction software (e.g. integrated into software localization tools) and easy online access to large quantities of texts.

From HT to FAHQT — Dimensions of translation automation

When dealing with the use of computers for translation, all kinds of acronyms are used to explain the different types of tools. A list of some of the more common ones, which readers can use as a quick self-test, includes: MT, CAT, HT, HAMT, MAHT, FAHQMT. Figure 2 puts these various acronyms into some kind of perspective.

The acronyms are now points on a continuum that shows the gradual increase in the automation of the translation process caused by the use of the tools

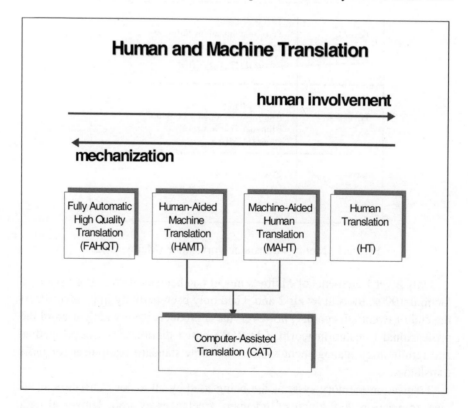

Figure 2. Dimensions of translation automation (from Hutchins & Somers 1992)

and the consequent decrease in human involvement. Let's take a closer look at this continuum.

It is quite obvious that both extremes shown in Figure 2 are easily discarded as valid models for contemporary translation. The antiquated image of a lone translator, armed only with a pencil or a typewriter and surrounded by dusty books, is no longer realistic. However, the idea of an independently acting, error-free translating machine is equally unrealistic and will not become a reality for a long time to come, if at all.

Having eliminated HT and FAHQT, our interest is focused on the area of translation where humans and computers co-operate to improve the overall quality of professional translation. Here, depending on whether humans or machines do the lion's share of a translation, we speak either of machine-aided human translation (MAHT) – translation aided by text-processing software, terminology databases or electronic dictionaries – or human-aided machine translation (HAMT) – translation memories (which come empty and initially have to be filled with translations from human translators) or MT systems that require extensive human pre- and post-editing.

Both terms, MAHT and HAMT, are often grouped together under the term computer-assisted translation (CAT).

The process-oriented approach

These two categorizations of electronic translation tools provide an understanding of the various degrees of functional and technological complexity involved. However, they do not really give us an in-depth understanding of the efficient and practical use of information and communication technology in professional translation activities. In order to obtain that understanding, a different approach is needed, an approach that sees electronic translation tools as an integral part of the translation process and as instruments that support the translator during the various sub-processes of translation.

Effective use of translation technology starts from the translator's position. In order to avoid a translational 'wag-the-dog' syndrome, the translator has to determine what types of translation technology are needed at what stages in the translation process in order to optimize his or her professional performance.

To use electronic tools effectively, and indeed to design and evaluate them, one must ensure compatibility between the tools and the steps that make up the translation process. This is especially important when using the abundant resources offered on the Internet. In preparation for this approach, we must examine translation both as a business and as a linguistic and cultural process.

Translation workflow management

Viewed as a business service, translation is not an isolated activity but is part of a larger process. Here we might consider the localization of a computer program, for which the translation of a user manual is just one of many subordinated processes. In such a scenario, the client's desire and the translator's task is to integrate the translation with the company's workflow as efficiently as possible. Establishing effective client–translator communication patterns is a rather simple process. Its framework consists of the reception of the source text and related information material and the subsequent delivery of the translated texts. Throughout the actual translating of the text, there can be various occasions for project-related client–translator communication (or translator–translator communication in the case of a team of translators collaborating on a project). Strategies have to be applied to guarantee a fast, secure, flexible and cost-efficient transfer of information between the partners involved in a translation process. The communication flow within a translation business model will be explained in detail in Chapter 2.

Supporting linguistic and cultural transfer

In addition to the organizational aspects of a translation project, translation technology is used to support what we might call the core process of a translation project: the cross-lingual and cross-cultural transfer of information. Here electronic translation tools function mostly as knowledge bases that provide the translator with world and expert knowledge.

Figure 3 shows the process model that James S. Holmes introduced for the evaluation of literary translations (Holmes 1988:84). Without going into the

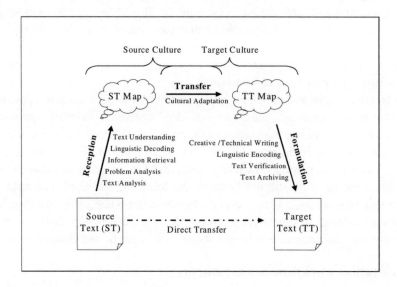

Figure 3. The translation process (based on Holmes 1988:84)

details, we can see how electronic tools can be used regardless of the type of text being translated. We have added some information to the model in order to show the sub-processes during the reception, transfer and formulation phases.

Holmes states that the reception of a source text leads to an abstract form, a mental concept of this text. He calls this a map. This abstraction is heavily influenced by contextual, intertextual, situational and individual factors. According to Holmes, the translator transforms the source text map into the target text map. In literary translations, but more frequently in technical texts, this step can involve a high degree of cross-cultural adaptation. The resulting mental image of the source text is then put into written form through a step that Holmes calls 'formulation'.

The three main elements in this process – reception, transfer and formulation – demand different competencies and activities by the translators, and different features by the tools used in their support.

Figure 4 replaces the sub-phases mentioned in the first model shown in Figure 3 with the tools that can be used to support the translation process. These tools will all be featured in this book.

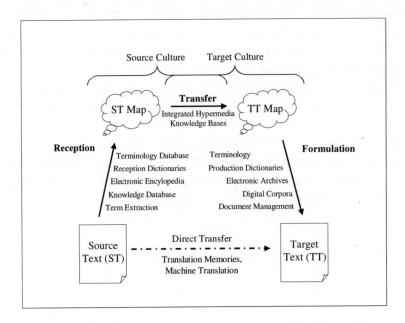

Figure 4. Electronic translation tools and the translation process

Let's take a closer look at these sub-processes and the different tools applicable to each.

The reception phase
During the reception phase of the translation process, the retrieval of (missing)

background knowledge plays a central role. As Brown & Yule point out, "understanding discourse is [...] essentially a process of retrieving stored information from memory and relating it to the encountered discourse" (Brown & Yule 1983:236). In order to understand the source text, world and domain knowledge, encyclopedias, knowledge databases and information retrieval systems are all equally important, as are the contacts to domain experts through newsgroups or mailing lists.

What else happens during the reception phase? The source text is analyzed, primarily with regard to functional aspects (Nord 1997) but also in order to discover the translator's information needs (Hönig 1998). This first step can also comprise an automated statistical text analysis which can be assisted by electronic tools such as Word Cruncher, WordSmith, or MonoConc or other terminology extraction tools, the aim being to filter the special terminology used in the text. This process can result in type-token lists, and in KWIC concordances showing the single term, the key word, in its context (Austermühl, Einhauser & Kornelius 1998). These lists can then be used by translators – especially a team of translators handling a large translation project – to ensure terminological consistency throughout the translation. The resulting KWIC concordances can also be directly imported into terminology databases such as MultiTerm or Microsoft Access, where further information and links to other resources can be added (Austermühl & Coners forthcoming).

Terminology databases or electronic dictionaries (either on CD-ROM or on the Internet) can then be used to decode the linguistic information of the source text. This kind of 'reception' dictionary – as opposed to the production (or encoding) dictionary used in the formulation phase – needs to provide a high degree of paradigmatic information, for example synonyms, antonyms and hyperonyms. Such dictionaries assist the understanding of the text-internal knowledge by positioning a given term within its lexical context.

The transfer phase

The transfer phase is a process unique to translation. Neither readers (whose activities match the reception phase of a translation) nor writers (who during the reception phase perform the same tasks as translators) share this phase. The adoption of the source text map to match the context of the target text culture is uniquely translational. It requires deep contrastive multicultural understanding and strong intercultural communication skills. The tools needed at this stage must offer a high degree of intercultural know-how, while at the same time providing the translator with comparative analysis of the cultures affected by the translation project.

Resources in this field are still rare; special kinds of dictionaries or terminology databases have to be designed to assist translators during the transfer phase. Here a thorough combination and network of linguistic, encyclopedic and intercultural knowledge is necessary. Elaborate terminology databases or hypermedia systems would seem to be valid solutions (Albrecht, Austermühl & Kornelius 1998). One of their advantages is the ability to incorporate not only textual information but also audio and video sequences, thereby giving lexicographers the opportunity to include non-verbal aspects in their works.

The formulation phase

The formulation phase confronts the translator with many challenges as far as the production of the target-language text is concerned. Here again, the use of dictionaries and terminology databases can support the translator quite effectively. The resources need to offer help with regard to syntagmatic relations of terms, as is done in many style guides (e.g. the German Stil-Duden) or in collocational dictionaries (such as the Collins Cobuild English Collocations on CD-ROM). Dictionaries that provide such information become valuable production tools. In addition to electronic dictionaries, the translator can turn to text corpora, such as those available on CD-ROM or on the Internet (e.g. using newspaper archives for the verification of certain expressions in the target language). Among the criteria these text archives have to fulfil are the provision of Boolean operators (AND, OR and NOT) and proximity operators (like NEAR, FOLLOWED BY or ADJACENT). These are even more important when locating collocations and determining the collocational range of any given combination.

Finally, the formulation or production phase should be followed by a document management process for storing the source and target texts in an electronic archive, and by importing the terminology used into a personal terminology management system (see Chapter 9). This post-translation phase could also include the editing of the translated texts for the application of a translation memory system.

Automating the translation process

The above model calls for individual use of electronic translation tools with regard to the specific sub-processes of the translation process. However, in the past 5 to 10 years the language industry has spent enormous amounts of money creating and marketing products that are able to cover the total translation process in one go. The products designed to automate the process of translation (almost) completely are translation memories, software localization tools and machine translation systems.

Translation memories

> Translation memory: A multilingual text archive containing (segmented, aligned, parsed and classified) multilingual texts, allowing storage and retrieval of aligned multilingual text segments against various search conditions.
> (Expert Advisory Group on Language Engineering Standards, EAGLES)

As the above definition states, translation memories such as IBM's Translation Manager, Atril's Déjà Vu, or Trados' Translator's Workbench are basically databases that allow the parallel storage of source and target text segments on a sentence, phrase or even word level. These segments can be retrieved in order to prepare for a new translation project. Special software identifies whether the text to be translated contains passages that are already stored in the translation memory (and therefore have already been translated). The translations found in the database are then offered to the user before the start of the new translation. Further, since phrases do not always look exactly alike (i.e. they are not *perfect* matches), translation memory software allows for so-called *fuzzy* matching. This technique searches the database for segments that are very similar to the original source text; it then presents the original translation used for those segments. The user can select the degree of acceptable 'fuzziness' in this pre-translation process.

Translation memories can be built either during or after the translation process. In the latter case, a process called alignment is used to match the text segments of the source-language text with their translations in the target text. This means that translations that have been produced prior to the purchase of a translation memory system can be 'recycled'. The alignment software, however, is rather expensive.

Software localization tools

Translation memory technology is an integral part of the latest line in automated translation products, namely software localization tools. These programs, such as Corel's Catalyst, provide several translation-related applications on one common platform. Depending on their configuration, localization tools integrate terminology extraction programs, automatic term look-up, translation memories and WYSIWIG ('what you see is what you get') editors, which are especially helpful when it comes to translating software messages, menus, dialogue boxes or command button labels. Chapter 9 will give a more detailed description of localization tools, including a case study involving Corel Catalyst.

Machine translation systems

Machine translation (MT) might be seen as the Holy Grail of computational linguistics. The basic idea of MT is that of Star Trek's universal translator or a mechanized version of Douglas Adams' Babel Fish – a black box that converts the source language input into a (perfect) target language output without any human interaction. After spending a great deal of money on the development of MT systems, researchers gave up the idea of Fully Automatic High-Quality Translation (FAHQT). They have instead focused on using MT for the translation of texts covering a highly restricted encyclopedic and terminological field and consisting of very simple sentence structures. Machine translation and modern MT systems are dealt with extensively in Chapter 10.

Tasks

✓ Define the following terms: globalization, digitization, glocalization.
✓ What does the acronym CAT stand for?
✓ What is a translation memory?
✓ What is the difference between HAMT and MAHT?
✓ Make a list of tools you consider to be electronic translation resources. Try to find their place within the model described in Figure 2.
✓ What kind of computer and network equipment does a modern translator need? How much do these products (i.e. hardware and software) cost?
✓ What are the relative advantages of electronic resources? What are the relative advantages of print media?

Further reading and Internet links

Austermühl, F. (forthcoming) Übersetzen im Informationszeitalter – Überlegungen zur Zukunft fachkommunikativen und interkulturellen Handelns im Global Village, Trier: WVT Wissenschaftlicher Verlag Trier.

Beck, U. (1998) *Was ist Globalisierung?* 5th edition, Frankfurt am Main: Suhrkamp.

McLuhan, M. and B.R. Powers (1989) The Global Village: Transformations in World Life and Media in the 21st Century, New York: Oxford University Press.

O'Hagan, M. (1996) The Coming Industry of Teletranslation: Overcoming Communication Barriers Through Telecommunication, Clevedon: Multilingual Matters.

Globalization Studies Homepage, Ruud Lubbers: http://www.globalize.org/ (Nov. 27, 2000).

UNESCO Observatory on the Information Society: http://www.unesco.org/webworld/observatory/doc_uni_access/multilingualism.html (Nov. 27, 2000).

2. Translator-client communication and information transfer

Since translation is a multi-billion-dollar industry, translating is very much a business process that requires appropriate professional conduct by the translator. This is especially true to the extent that the translation of any given text is just part of a wider business process. For example, the translation of a computer manual from English into Spanish is perhaps part of the complete global localization of a US$5,000 business software program that involves 23 target languages and cultures.

As was pointed out in the previous chapter, in a globalized economy almost no business transaction can be implemented without first addressing the need for linguistic and cultural adaptation. This need becomes especially clear when looking at the software sector. Here, the importance of the time-to-market factor is demonstrated by the aim of 'SimShip', i.e. the simultaneous international shipping of all target-market versions of a specific software product.

As far as the localization and translation of the software is concerned, enormous organization is demanded of the project management and translation teams. As a professional translator involved in a SimShip project – no matter how small or large your contribution – you have specific responsibilities that have little to do with the content of your work or its strictly translational quality. Try putting yourself in the position of a project manager of an international agency in charge of translating the manual for a software product to be released in 20 countries. For this release, the manual has to be translated into 16 languages; all language versions are scheduled to be shipped at the same time. As project manager, you have given tasks to local translators or translator teams. Overall you will be sending text and background information to a great number of different translators, and you will be receiving translations from them. You will provide all translators with glossaries, versions of older manuals, the new software itself and an elaborate style guide. The translators, on the other hand, will be regularly sending you questions regarding the text to be translated, questions that you have to pass on to the experts from the company that produced the software. All kinds of expected and unexpected organizational problems will occur (glossary updates or changes, additions to the original text, etc.). How will you structure your work? What kind of general organizational decisions will you take? How will you communicate with the translators? And above all, what will you expect your translators to do and not do?

The use of e-mail, FTP and WWW-based working groups

In a translation project, the overall goal of the co-operative effort between translators and clients is to implement a communication strategy that minimizes
translation time (and thus costs) while at the same time producing high-quality
work. In addition, an easy, flexible, fast and secure exchange of information is
needed to maximize client satisfaction. This is especially important when we
bear in mind that translation has become a tele-profession, where team members may be spread all over the world. Figure 5 shows the basic workflow in a
translation project. The individual steps will be explained below.

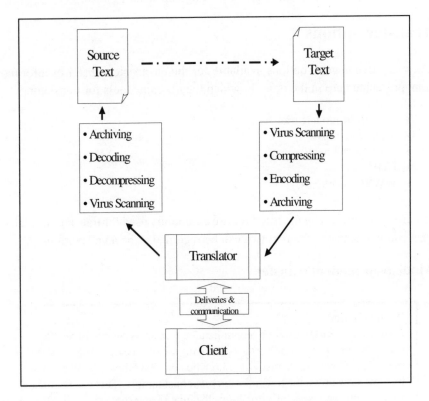

Figure 5. Workflow in a translation project

Traditional forms of order handling via fax or paper-and-envelope mail
('snail mail') simply cannot meet all the above criteria. They are too slow and
expensive; they are thus declining in importance. The increasing digitization of
data has created a primarily electronic exchange of source and target texts. This
first happened on floppy disks, then increasingly through the use of file transfer through modem-to-modem connection or ISDN lines. International data

networks are now regularly used to send texts as e-mail file attachments. The most recent text transfer options now include the downloading of files from a client's Internet site via FTP (File Transfer Protocol, an Internet service that makes the exchange of files over the Internet possible), and the use of websites for distributing text files.

Because of the decreasing use of mail and fax services, here we will be concentrating on the ways data can be exchanged online, i.e. through electronic transmission, as opposed to offline exchange where the medium on which the data are encoded (e.g. paper or a floppy disk) has to be physically transferred.

Let us now take a closer look at various forms of electronic data exchange, the way they work, and their respective advantages and disadvantages. We will then discuss tools for compressing, encoding and securing files.

Transfer options

There are five general options available for the electronic transfer of information, presented here in the order in which they became tools for translators:

- modem-to-modem transfer;
- ISDN file transfer;
- e-mail attachments;
- FTP;
- WWW downloads.

In current practice, only the last three are commonly used for translation-related data communication. The first two can be regarded as backup solutions.

Modem-to-modem transfer

> What you need:
> *Hardware*: A modem with a recommended transmission rate of 56 Kbps (thousand bits per second — these modems are often called 56K or V.90 modems). Slower modems with 33.6 Kbps or 28.8 Kbps will also work but will slow down the transmission rate considerably. This can become very expensive, especially for long-distance or international calls. Remember that the maximum speed also depends on the abilities of the receiving modem (see below).
> *Software*: Communications software that controls the modem in use, enables a connection to be set up between sender and receiver, and helps you manage the exchange of files. There are many such programs on the market, for example the shareware program Telix, which can be downloaded as a free demo version at ftp://ftp.cdrom.com/pub/garbo/garbo_pc/termprog/telix351.zip.

In this scenario, the sender and receiver of data are directly connected with each other via telephone lines. Modems connect the users' PC with the telephone network. The term *modem* derives from the words **mo**dulator/**dem**odulator which describe the workings of the device. A modem transforms the computer's digital signal into an analogue signal so that it can be transferred over the telephone network, which is usually analogue. This transformation process is called modulation. At the receiving end, a modem reverses the process and transforms (i.e. demodulates) the analogue signals coming over the telephone networks into digital signals that can be processed by the computer (see Figure 6).

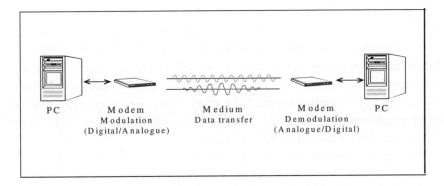

Figure 6. Modem-to-modem connection

The connection between the two computers is implemented by one computer using a modem and software to call the other computer over the telephone network (the same way that one fax machine calls another to send a facsimile). Once the computers are connected (i.e. once the phone call is in progress) data can be exchanged in the form of files. A translation in WinWord format, a list of questions in a 123 datasheet or a terminology database can thus be sent over the phone line in any direction. The initiation of the phone call and the handling of the file exchange is controlled by specific data-transfer software, for example HyperTerminal (part of the Windows operating system), or by the shareware program Telix.

The speed of the data transmission depends on the speed supported by the modems used. At the moment the top speed for modem-to-modem transfer is 56 Kbps but this is achieved only if both modems support that transfer rate. If the transfer rates supported by the two modems differ, the speed drops to that of the slower modem. In the future, the transmission speed of modem-to-modem data exchange might increase significantly through the spread of XDSL modems, which offer significantly faster transmission rates.

A modem-to-modem connection is basically the same as the connection you use to dial up your Internet Service Provider (ISP) via a modem. Here, too, your modem calls another modem to establish a connection that then is used for the exchange of data. In direct data exchanges between modems, the selection of files to be transferred and the technical settings can sometimes be more complicated than they are in the case of ISPs. However, since a direct connection between modems is mostly only used as a contingency plan to fall back on, you should not worry too much about those details right now. You should simply be aware of this option in case a client demands it or if you have to request it from a client.

Advantages and disadvantages of modem connections

The main advantage of using a modem for file transmission is that it requires minimal resources. For example, if both sides use Windows, they can use HyperTerminal as the communications software and no more than a modem will be needed to complete the transfer. No ISP or e-mail account is needed, and once the right parameters for the data exchange have been established, transferring files is merely a matter of routine. Some clients actually prefer the direct transfer of files, often for reasons of security. In any case, you should always ask about a client's transfer preferences.

Nevertheless, there are several reasons why a modem-to-modem connection should not be your prime choice for translation-related data communication and file exchange.

In terms of cost, modem-to-modem connections sharply increase your communication expenses if used for transmitting large files to a geographically distant receiver. In such cases you have to pay the cost of a long-distance or international phone call for the duration of the transmission. And since the duration depends on the speed of the modems used, anything below a 56K modem will be slow and therefore expensive. Transmission costs can nevertheless be reduced by using file compression (see below).

Modem-to-modem connections also reduce the flexibility of the data exchange. In order to connect to a client's modem, both PCs have to be switched on, as do the respective modems, and the communications software must be running. Unless the receiving end has all three components (computer, modem, communications software) running 24 hours a day, 7 days a week, which for security reasons alone is not to be recommended, both communication partners have to agree on a time for the exchange to take place.

The relative stability of the transmission also has to be taken into consideration. The longer a transmission by telephone takes, the more likely a break in the connection, and that will interrupt the current file transmission. In such cases you have to re-establish the connection with the receiving side. Then you either resume the transmission at the point of failure or start the transmission all over again.

Exchanging data via ISDN

What you need:

Hardware: Access to the ISDN provided by a basic rate interface (BRI) or a higher bandwidth primary rate interface (PRI), as well as an ISDN adapter to connect your PC to the digital telephone net.

Software: A communications software program that sets up the connection between sender and receiver, and helps you manage the exchange of files. Most ISDN adapters come with a communications package that includes a file transfer program. The program should support the Euro File Transfer (EFT) protocol.

The integrated services digital network (ISDN) is basically a digital, multifunctional telephone network allowing both speech and data transmission over digital lines. In the United States, ISDN is mostly used for fast Internet access only, but it is widespread in most Western European countries, where it is quickly replacing analogue telephone networks.

ISDN comes in two sizes, the basic rate interface (BRI) offering a total transmission rate of 144 Kbps, and the primary rate interface (PRI), which provides a combined transfer rate of up to 2 Mbps (million bits per second). The PRI, which offers up to 30 different channels, is mostly used for corporate communications. The smaller bandwidth BRI is nevertheless a very effective communication solution for private individuals and for SOHO situations (SOHO: Small Office, Home Office).

A BRI offers two communication channels (these are called B channels) that can be used for digital voice, fax, video or data transmissions, and one D channel that controls the data exchange on the B channels. Both B channels offer a transmission rate of 64 Kbps and can be combined via a process called bonding or channel bundling, giving a total speed of 128 Kbps.

The presence of two separate channels makes it possible to conduct a phone conversation on one channel while using the other to send a fax, for example, or (perhaps if the conversation is getting too boring) to surf the Internet. Individually or combined, the B channels can also be used for data transmission. They are thus a viable option for sending translation-related files.

How does file transfer using an ISDN connection work? As in the modem-to-modem scenario, a computer is connected to another computer, but now via ISDN. As a prerequisite, both computers have to be connected to the digital telephone network (the monthly fees are generally higher than those for an analogue connection). The technical connection with the computer is implemented using an ISDN adapter. Since both the computer and the telephone network use digital signals, the ISDN adapter has much less work to do than a modem (the transformation from analogue to digital signals and vice versa does not take place). Setting up a connection between computers is thus much faster using ISDN adapters than with modems. The noisy first contact between modems (the so-called 'handshake') does not happen in ISDN transmission. This leads to shorter transmission times (and costs). Besides the ISDN adapter, communications software is needed to manage the dial-up process and the exchange of files. ISDN adapters usually come equipped with software packages, so you probably already have the software needed for the transmission. The exchange of files using ISDN is widely standardized (based on the EFT – Euro File Transfer – protocol), so compatibility between sender and receiver is not a problem.

Thanks to its higher transmission speed and faster dial-up process, ISDN offers much better performance than do modem connections. As mentioned, if the two B channels are combined you can transfer files at a rate of 128 Kbps. The bonding is managed by the communications software and has to be supported by the receiving partner. At this speed, simple videoconferences can be carried out using the connection.

ISDN offers a fast and reliable method for transferring files, especially in Europe where its use is quite widespread. Nevertheless, it is still a way of transferring files by establishing a direct connection with your communication partner over a telephone line – that is, at the cost of a regular phone call. For long-distance and international calls, this can be extremely cost-intensive, especially when combining channels, and this factor should be taken into consideration. Also, the computer and communications programs have to be running at the time of the transmission, which reduces both your flexibility and that of your client.

Communicating through electronic mail

The sending and receiving of electronic mail (e-mail) is clearly the most widely used Internet service. Its general advantages of speed, flexibility and cost-effectiveness make electronic mail a perfect communication tool for translators as well, and it has indeed become the translation industry's foremost transfer solution. The ability to attach files to the electronic messages can be used to exchange texts or glossaries between translator and client, or to send questions and remarks to other translators.

What you need:
To send e-mail over the Internet (e-mail also works within local area networks (LANs) and within online services; it's even simpler there) you will need to be connected to the Internet (using your Internet Service Provider and a modem, ISDN or LAN access). A LAN is a small computer network, mostly confined to a single building or group of buildings. In addition, you will need a software program – an e-mail 'client ' – in order to write, send, receive and read text messages and attached files.

E-mailing is a rather routine and automated task. Since you only need a limited number of features to send and receive e-mails and file attachments, it is a very easy way to communicate with your clients and colleagues all over the world. The software features you are most likely to use with e-mail are:

- entering e-mail addresses
- working with address books
- writing text messages to one recipient (offline)
- writing text messages to numerous recipients (offline)
- attaching a file to a text message
- attaching numerous files to a text message
- sending several e-mails at a time
- receiving e-mails
- scanning e-mails for computer viruses
- downloading all received e-mails
- extracting attached files
- replying to e-mails
- forwarding e-mails
- downloading and archiving e-mails.

Some e-mail basics

An e-mail usually consists of the following basic components:

The recipient's address (e.g. juan.ramirez@tradu.es or susanna.smith@ compuserve.com): E-mail addresses are standardized. From right to left they show:

- the top-level domain, i.e. a country code such as *.de*, *.es* or *.it*, for Germany, Spain or Italy respectively — addresses in the United States do not have a specific country code assigned — or the domain as such, where *.com* shows a commercial origin and *.org* to indicates that the server is a non-profit organization;
- the institution that a recipient belongs to or the server that they use. Domains will be explained in detail in Chapter 3;
- the @ symbol (pronounced *at* in English);
- the code or name of the recipient, which can also include the first name, generally separated by a dot (.).

When sending an e-mail you can enter multiple addresses by separating them using commas or semicolons.

A subject or reference (re.) line: This is used to briefly describe the contents of the message that follows. Messages do not appear as full text in your incoming mailbox but only as a listing of the sender's name, the time and date of receipt and this subject line. In business mails it is important to be precise and informative with regard to the contents of this field. The user will first browse their in-box, looking at the subject line and the senders; they will then select the messages to be read first. So if you have an urgent message for somebody, start the subject line with URGENT and then state the nature of your emergency. But do not use this strategy all the time; otherwise your 'urgent' messages may soon be ignored.

cc: cc stands for *carbon copy*, which means that copies of your mail will be sent to the people whose e-mail addresses you enter in this field. The cc addresses will appear in the header of the received mail.

bcc: bcc stands for *blind carbon copy*. This line also contains the names of people to whom you will be sending copies of the mail. However, unlike the cc line, the recipients' addresses will not show in the message header. Thus, the recipients specified in the address field and the cc line will not know that a message was sent to these addresses.

Body: The 'body' of an e-mail is the text message that you type into the respective field. Although only plain ASCII characters used to be accepted as part of a message, these days most e-mail clients allow you to use special characters (like *ñ* or *ë*) and even special formatting (bold, italics, block alignment). However, due to some difficulties in transferring these characters and formatting options over the Internet, I recommend keeping the message format as simple as possible, perhaps even avoiding the use of accents or umlaut vowels (in German *ü* and *ä* can also be written *ue* and *ae*). Also, try to keep your text messages short and precise. Longer texts should be sent in word-processing format as attachments.

Attachment: To send files such as longer texts, glossaries or images, you should add the files as 'attachments'. You can send several files (in any format) as attachments at the same time.

In order to make your e-mail communication more effective and – if you are using a phone connection instead of a network connection – less expensive, you should always compose your messages offline. Once they are finished, you can dial up your ISP and send all outgoing mails in one go, receiving all incoming e-mails at the same time. All major e-mail clients offer a feature that makes sending and receiving numerous e-mails an automatic operation.

There are numerous e-mail clients available, offering a wide range of functions, but they mostly work the same way. Here we will concentrate on two widely used clients and the functions you are most likely to need for a translation project. The software packages to be dealt with are Netscape Messenger and AOL Mail.

Using online services for e-mail – the case of AOL
America Online (AOL) is the world's largest online service. An online service offers a variety of exclusive services and resources to members who pay a monthly fee. In addition to this restricted use, AOL and other online services

(CompuServe, Microsoft Network, T-Online, Prodigy etc.) offer a gateway to the Internet so that members can send e-mails or surf the worldwide web.

AOL uses a specific, proprietary e-mail client that is part of their installation package. You can also access your mail service via AOL's Internet site (www.aol.com). That way you can receive your mail from any Internet terminal anywhere in the world. In this case the AOL software does not have to be installed on the computer you use. If you are not an AOL member you can download their software from AOL's website or get it on one of the many freely distributed CD-ROMs. At AOL's website you will also find information on free trial memberships. After you have started AOL, sending an e-mail is very easy (shown here with version 5.0).

1. Click on Mail Center, Write Mail.
2. In the Send To box, enter the address of the recipient. Separate multiple recipients using commas. You can also add addresses from your address book.
3. If desired, add further recipients in the Copy To box. Separate multiple copy recipients using commas. You can also add addresses from your address book.
4. Enter a subject in the Subject line.
5. Enter the message.
6. In order to attach a file to the message, click on Attachments/Attach and select the file you want to attach. To attach multiple files, just repeat this process as many times as needed. Multiple file attachments will be encoded automatically by AOL using the MIME format (see below).
7. Click Send Later to save the message. The message will be stored for future delivery. If you are already online – that is, connected to AOL – you can now send the mail by clicking Send Now.
8. Compose other e-mails if you want. When you have finished all the e-mails that you want to send, connect to AOL. Once you are online, a message will pop up on the screen informing you that you have stored e-mails. At that point you can send all the e-mails at once.

Anyone who has seen Meg Ryan and Tom Hanks knows how AOL tells you, 'You've got mail', at least as far as the American version of the software is concerned. In the German version of AOL an envelope is used to indicated new mail arrivals instead of the US-style letter box. In any case, you just click on the symbol to see the list of your new mails. Double-clicking on a mail in the list brings up the full message text.

To reply to a mail, click on the Reply button. A new window will open, displaying a message in which the recipient's address has already been filled in. The reference line used in the mail you are replying to has also already been entered.

In order to forward a mail to someone else, just click on the Forward button and enter the e-mail address of the person you want to forward the mail to. You can enter your comments before sending the mail, or you can forward it without adding further information.

If the mail you have just received has a file attached to it, you can download the attachment right away by clicking on the Download Now button. You can also save the file for later download by clicking on the Download Later button.

If you want to save the message you have received, simply choose File/Save.

To make the uploading (sending) and downloading (receiving) of e-mails faster, use Automatic AOL. This will allow you to work on your e-mails offline. You can configure the messenger service by clicking Mail Center/Set up Automatic AOL.

Using Netscape Messenger

If you are not using an online service with a proprietary e-mail client, you can access the Internet and its service using an ISP which lets you use an e-mail client of your choice. In this case you will be using a commercial e-mail client for communicating, most likely one of the following:

- Netscape Messenger
- Microsoft Outlook
- Pegasus Mail
- Eudora.

Outlook is the personal information management component of the Microsoft Office family of products. In addition to offering address, time and project management features, it also serves as a fax machine and an e-mail client. Outlook Express is a boiled-down version of Outlook, offering only its communications features. Pegasus and Eudora are two widely used e-mail clients. See http://www.pegasus.com and http://www.eudora.com for more information. Here we will briefly describe how to use Netscape Messenger.

Netscape Messenger is the e-mail client that is part of the Netscape Communicator software package (which also includes the WWW browser Netscape Navigator). Check Netscape's website at http://www.netscape.com to find out how to get Netscape Communicator.

When you first use an e-mail client, you will have to open an account. This means you have to configure the software, telling it your name, your e-mail address, the e-mail address you want replies to be sent to (which will usually, but not necessarily, be your regular e-mail address). In addition you will have to tell the software your user name, the address of the computer in which your ISP stores your incoming mails (POP 3 or IMAP), which server is used for outgoing mails (SMTP), and what kind of mail server is used. In Netscape Messenger, all this information is put in the Preferences file (select it at the bottom of the Edit menu), under Mail & Groups. Your ISP will be able to give you all the information necessary to set up the mail program. You will only have to fill in this information once.

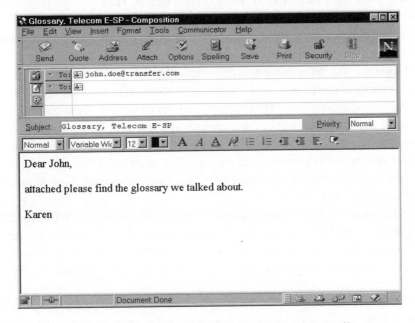

Figure 7. Netscape Messenger - Composing new mail

To compose a message with Netscape Messenger, click on the New Msg symbol. A new message window opens. Type in the address information, the reference line text and the message text. Click on the Attach symbol to add a file (or multiple files) to this message. Select the file from the dialogue box that appears. To add more than one file to a message press down the Ctrl key and click on each file you want to add. The paper clip indicating the presence or absence of a file attachment will shift from blue (no attachment) to red (one or more files attached). If you want to detach the file from the message, simply select the file and hit Delete on your keyboard.

If you want to check for new mails, just click on the Get Msg symbol. All new mails will be transferred to your in-box. Attached files will be marked by a paper clip symbol. Just click on the filename at the end of the message, and choose a file location to download the file to. By clicking on the address of the sender you can add this e-mail address to your local address book.

If you want to reply to a mail, click on Reply (or, if the mail you are replying to had more than one recipient, click on Reply to all). A new mail window will open. The address and subject information will already have been filled in. Type in your reply and click on the Send button. If you would like to forward the

mail you are reading, simply click on the Forward button. A new mail window
will open. Fill in the address information of the recipient, add a comment if you
want to, and click on Send.

Using FTP and the WWW to receive clients' files

With the digitization of products, more and more clients have turned to the
Internet not only to communicate with their partners but also to exchange goods
and services. The same thing is happening in the field of translation: many clients make their source texts and additional information material available on an
FTP or worldwide web (WWW) server. In both cases, the client posts the respective files on the server. All you have to do is use your WWW browser (e.g.
Netscape Navigator or Microsoft's Internet Explorer), enter the URL for the
server and the file you are looking for, and click on the files that are designated
for you. You will then be prompted to select a location on your computer where
you would like to store the file.

FTP stands for File Transfer Protocol, an Internet service used for transferring files. Using FTP you can, for example, download a selection of glossaries
containing Microsoft's standard terminology. To do so, you enter the address
ftp://ftp.microsoft.com/developr/msdn/newup/glossary/ into the address field of
your browser and hit Enter.

The glossaries are made available in the form of self-extracting archive files.
This means that once you have downloaded the information onto your computer, you can open the archive and extract the files by simply double-clicking on
the filename in the Explorer window. Note that the files are generally very large
in size, which means that the transfer process may take some time. Select the
language of your choice (there are only language pairs available, with English
always being one of the two languages), and just click on the file.

Downloading a file from a WWW server works in much the same way. The
file is made available in the form of a hyperlink. All you have to do is go to the
respective webpage, look for a hyperlink for the file, and click on the hyperlink.
You will then be prompted to save the file on your local computer.

Optimizing online file transfer

Getting files to and from your client is just one part of your digital workflow.
You should also make sure the transfer of data is secure, fast and flexible.

The security of your file transfer (and of the computer system that you use
for the file transfer) can be severely threatened by computer viruses. To avoid
being infected, you will have to install a virus scanner on your computer and
keep it up to date. Security breaches can also occur when an unauthorized person reads your mail or accesses your computer. The latter can be secured by

using passwords (which should be changed on a regular basis). Check your computer manual on how to protect your system with passwords. If you only want selected persons to read your mail and the attached files, you can make your files inaccessible to outsiders by a process called encryption. To do so, you need special software such as the well-known program Pretty Good Privacy (PGP). More information on PGP can be found at http://www.pgp.com. If you are regularly receiving confidential data (e.g. contracts) you should definitely acquire some reliable encryption software. In any case, you should talk to your clients about what kind of security measures they consider necessary.

Scanning files for viruses

A computer virus is a program designed to destroy data on the computer systems that it infects or to bring the system's operation to a halt. Viruses are transported between computers in files distributed online or on diskettes; they can infect other files and programs. Many of today's viruses are 'macro' viruses, which means they are disguised in the form of a macro, for example in WinWord. If you receive a file infected with a macro virus and open it, the virus can spread and embed itself in future documents that you create with that application. Due to the high volume of Word document transfer among translators, their computers are prime targets for macro viruses. A 'Trojan Horse' is very similar to a virus. Disguised as a useful program, it tries to enter your computer system and can cause damage to it. Unlike a virus, a Trojan horse does not automatically replicate itself.

Extensive information on viruses can be found on various Internet sites, for example in the virus encyclopedia at http://www.avp.ch/avpve/.

To avoid being infected by computer viruses and to make sure you are sending uninfected files to your clients (who would then soon be ex-clients), you need to install an anti-virus program. This utility searches for viruses on your computer, diskettes or incoming files, and can also disinfect infected files.

For greater effectiveness you should add the anti-virus program (they are also called 'virus scanners') to your Autostart folder. Also, since new viruses are reported on a daily basis, make sure you update your anti-virus program regularly. Most programs have an automatic update function that will remind you to get the latest features.

There is an enormous variety of virus scanners available. Go to http://download.cnet.com and click Utilities/Antivirus for a list of virus scanners. Here we will just look at one example.

McAfee VirusScan is an anti-virus product made by Network Associates. You can download a free evaluation copy from the McAfee website at http://www.mcafee.com. To scan your computer's hard disks or a floppy disk, start McAfee and tell it which disks or which parts of the disks to scan.

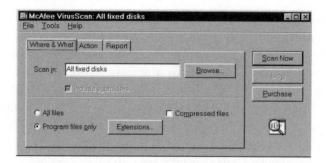

Figure 8. McAfee – Selecting files to be scanned

As Figure 8 shows, you can configure McAfee so that it scans only selected drives or folders (see the Scan In box). You can also specify the format of the files to be scanned (All files, Program files, e.g. with .exe or .doc extensions) and you can include compressed (zipped) files in the scanning procedure.

Click Scan Now to start the virus search. If the virus scanner finds an infected file, it displays a message prompting you to either clean the file or to delete it right away. Click the Clean button to disinfect the file. If the program is successful, McAfee will display a message confirming that the file has been cleaned.

File compression

They say time is money. In terms of data transmission, size is time, therefore size is money. To be more explicit: the larger the file to be transferred over a network, the longer it will take (provided that the speed of the transmission channel stays unchanged). If you are accessing the Internet via a telephone network, any prolongation of the transfer process will almost certainly cost you more money. Further, as we have noted, the longer the transmission, the more likely a transmission failure.

The solution to this problem is to make the files smaller. This process is called *file compression*, generally also referred to as *zipping*. Zipping is especially useful for large graphic or sound files, but is also quite efficient with Word documents, spreadsheets or databases. File compression programs look for data redundancies in a file and eliminate them to help reduce the overall size. A compressed file can be handled for transmission, for example as an e-mail attachment, like any other file. On the recipient's side, the file has to be decompressed using a zip program that supports the format in which the original file was compressed.

In addition to reducing file sizes, a compression program enables you to combine several individual files into one compressed file, often referred to as an archive file or zip file. Although most e-mail clients allow you to attach several files to a message, sometimes this feature is implemented in a user-unfriendly and unsafe way. By first compressing several files into one archive file, the process of attaching numerous files can become considerably less time consuming. Furthermore, zipping a file or several files before transferring them over the Internet can reduce problems with the representation of special characters (see Chapter 3).

Among the many compression software products available, the program WinZip is probably the best known. An evaluation version of WinZip can be downloaded from http://www.winzip.com.

Of the many features that WinZip offers, only two will most likely be of immediate interest to you: compressing a file or several files before transmission, and decompressing a received archive file.

Compressing files with WinZip

When installed, WinZip automatically integrates its features into the Explorer menu (in Windows 95, 98 and NT). This makes it very simple to use. Compressing a file with WinZip is actually as easy as one, two, three (if the file you want to compress is located on your desktop you can go directly to step 2).

1. Start Explorer and open the folder in which the file to be compressed is located.
2. Right click on the file you want to compress.
3. Select Add to Filename.zip, and acknowledge the licence agreement.

That's it. The new archive is automatically added to the folder in which you are working. In order to compress several files at a time, follow the steps below.

1. Start Explorer and open the folder in which the file to be compressed is located.
2. Select the files you want to compress (press the Ctrl key while you click on each file).
3. Right-click on the selected files.
4. In the context menu choose Add to Zip. This starts up WinZip.
5. In the Add dialogue box select New to add an (empty) archive to the shown folder.
6. Select a location for the new archive and enter a filename. Click on the OK button to confirm your selection.
7. Click on Add to start the file compression.
8. The compressed files are shown in the WinZip window. The Size column shows their original sizes, the Packed column shows their sizes after compression. The Ratio column indicates the percentage by which the fields have been compressed. The combined size of the original files (770 Kb) is

shown in the WinZip status bar. The overall size of the new archive (324 Kb) can be checked in the Explorer window. As you can see, in Figure 10 the files were compressed by about 58 percent.

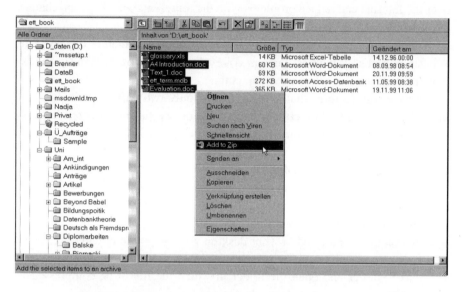

Figure 9. WinZip - Compressing multiple files in Explorer

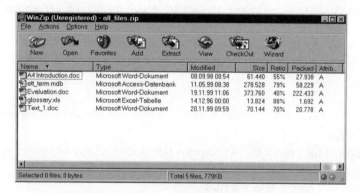

Figure 10. WinZip - List of archived files

Adding files to an existing archive

If you want to add new files to an existing zip file, all you have to do in Explorer (or on your computer desktop) is drag the file you want to add from its original location and drop it on the existing archive. The file will automatically be added. This way you can replace an old file in the archive with a new updated version.

Deleting files from an archive

If you want to delete a file from an existing archive, you will first have to open the archive by double-clicking on it in Explorer or on the desktop. In the WinZip window you can then select the respective file and then delete it by hitting the Delete key on your keyboard. You will be asked if you want to delete only the selected file, all files or other files that you can specify here. Click Delete to confirm your selection.

Opening an archive
If you have received a zip file containing, for example, the files that make up the source text for a translation project, you will have to open and extract them. Here again, using the Explorer is the easiest solution (if the file you want to unzip is located on your desktop you can go directly to step 2).

1. After you have downloaded the archive file, open the folder in which it is located in Explorer.
2. Right-click on the archive file.
3. Select the command Extract to folder X:\foldername\foldername\zip_ filename (X is the drive letter), in this case D:\Mails\In_Box\all_files.
4. WinZip extracts all files and automatically puts them into a new folder in their original formats. The folder name is identical to the name of the zip file.

Checking the contents of an archive
If you want to see what files and archives contain before extracting them, simply double-click on the filename in the Explorer window or on the desktop. WinZip will then show all files compressed in the archive. By selecting files from this list and then clicking on the Extract symbol you can extract individual files from the archive.

Beware of zipped viruses
Do not forget that archive files (or the files they contain) can also be infected by viruses. Almost all virus scanners let you analyze zip files. Just make sure that you have activated the respective option in your anti-virus program.

Encoding and decoding files

You may have received e-mail attachments that have strange-looking filename extensions like .mim, .uue or .bin. These extensions indicate that the file you received has been *encoded*. This can be for two reasons. First, when you enclose a file in an e-mail the software usually encodes it, which means it turns the specific data into a plain ASCII text that can then be transferred over the network. Many e-mail systems do this automatically, so the person who sent you the file might not even know their files were encoded. A second reason for encoding files is to make sure that the character sets that you are using in your message and your files stay unchanged. So if you have already had problems with keeping your ç, å, ü, ñ, and ì alive during a transmission over the Internet, try encoding them. An encoded file has to be decoded at the recipient's end by using the same encoding scheme. The most popular format for this kind of file encoding is MIME, short for Multipurpose Internet Mail Extensions.

There are several software products that allow you to encode and decode files. But if you already have used WinZip, you do not need to bother looking for specific encoding/decoding software. WinZip can open (decode) files encoded in formats such as MIME, UUencoded, XXencoded, or BinHex MIME files. WinZip is also able to encode your files using the UUE format. However, in most cases simply zipping the file will be enough to get all the information to the recipient in one piece. Only if you are experiencing problems, either with multimedia files or with character sets, should you turn to special encoding and decoding software.

In order to decode a file with WinZip, simply double-click on the encoded file in Explorer. This will automatically start up WinZip. Here, you can extract the files just as you would extract files from a WinZip archive.

In addition to WinZip, it might be useful to have some other encoding software available (e.g. WinEncoder or Fastcode). Search for 'encoding software' at http://download.cnet.com to find out what programs are available for download.

Tasks

✓ What options are generally available for the transfer of data within a translation project?
✓ What does a 'zip' program do?
✓ What are the advantages of electronic data transfer? What are the specific advantages of e-mail? What security hazards do you see?
✓ Go to Microsoft's FTP server and download the MS glossary for your native language.
✓ What is a 'Trojan Horse'?
✓ Download Winzip's and McAfee's latest evaluation versions.
✓ Compress a couple of files and send them as e-mail attachments to a colleague. Make sure to scan for viruses.

Further reading and Internet links

Gurian, Phil (1996) *E-mail Business Strategies*, Spokane: Grand National Press.
Hughes, Lawrence E. (1998) *Internet E-mail: Protocols, Standards, and Implementation* (Artech House Telecommunications Library), Norwood: Artech House.

Rudolph, Mark T. (1998) *Correo electrónico qué fácil*, Barcelona: Marcombo Editorial.

Sprung, R.C. (ed.) (2000) *Translating Into Success. Cutting-edge strategies for going multilingual in a global age.* American Translators Association Scholarly Monograph Series. Volume XI. Amsterdam & Philadelphia: John Benjamins.

Tunstall, Joan (1996) *Better, Faster Email: Getting the Most Out of Email*, St. Leonards: Allen & Unwin.

America Online: http://www.aol.com
CNET (software download): http://download.cnet.com
Computer virus encyclopedia: http://www.avp.ch/avpve
Eudora (e-mail client): http://www.eudora.com
McAfee (anti-virus software): http://www.mcafee.com
Netscape: http://www.netscape.com
Pegasus (e-mail client): http://www.pmail.com
Pretty Good Privacy (encryption software): http://www.pgp.com
WinZip (archiving software): http://www.winzip.com

3. Translation and the Internet

The Internet, a global network of computers, has brought about radical changes in the way people all around the world – or better, those in the industrialized world – are working and communicating. It is also significantly affecting the way translators work today, not only in the way they handle orders but also in how they search for linguistic and encyclopedic information. The way the Internet is changing the research habits of translators can be called a paradigm shift. In view of this importance, the next three chapters will deal extensively with the global computer network and the resources it has to offer.

This chapter will explain the technological structure of the Internet and the basic workings of its multimedia offspring, the worldwide web. Chapter 4 will describe strategies for information research and quality evaluation. Chapter 5 presents selected translation-related online resources.

The basics of the Internet

To understand what the Internet is, it is important to distinguish between its technological infrastructure and the services that make use of that infrastructure.

The network infrastructure

Let's start with the technical side of the Internet. It is basically a computer network, albeit a rather large one. A network is by definition a combination of intersecting or interconnecting filaments, lines, passages, etc. A computer network is no different. As soon as you connect two computers with a cable you have created a computer network, no matter what kind of computer and what kind of cable you are using.

In the case of the Internet, there are quite a lot of computers connected within a global network. At the time of writing, in 2000, there are hundreds of millions of computers connected to the Internet. The interesting thing is that the computers that are part of the Internet (and which, by using the Internet, can communicate with one another) are of all types, sizes, brands and ages. And they are all spread all over the world. The Internet can be categorized as a Global Area Network (GAN). Its heterogeneous computer family can comprise a small laptop computer in Alaska or a huge, building-sized super-computer in Okinawa, an old 286 in a Moscow basement or a brand-new Pentium III in a German university (or the other way round, to paint a more realistic picture). Nor does it matter whether the computers use Unix or Windows or any other operating system, or whether they are Macs or belong to the IBM tribe. It is also irrelevant whether the scripts used to operate the computers run from left to right, from right to left, in both directions or from top to bottom. All computers form part of the same planet-spanning network; they are all able to get in touch and communicate with each other. The various modes of communication are described below.

The computers on the Internet are either 'host' (or server) computers or 'client' computers. The host computers are usually more powerful than the client computers. These servers contain the data and information that can be transferred to the user's computer, the client. (Note that the terms 'client' and 'server' refer to not only the hardware but also the software of the respective computers.)

What makes the Internet work is the fact that all the different computers are able to understand each other. This is made possible by something called TCP/IP (Transmission Control Protocol/Internet Protocol), which is a communications protocol (or rather a set of numerous protocols) that works as the 'mother tongue' of the Internet network. A protocol is basically a set of rules defining a format for the data to be transferred and the mode of the transfer.

The computers are connected to each other through a variety of transmission media. The most popular transmission media are twisted-pair wire cables (the normal electrical wire that most phone lines are made of), coaxial cables (the type of cable used for cable television), and fibre optic cables (cables made out of glass). The Internet also uses wireless transmission paths in the form of terrestrial (i.e. cellular) and satellite radio.

The history of the Internet

The birth of the Internet can be traced back to the heyday of the Cold War. In its effort to create a decentralized computer communications network that would prove safe against a nuclear attack, the Rand Cooperation, a Washington-based think-tank, came up with the idea of a centreless network consisting of multiple, equally important computers or nodes. This network was to be able to transfer information to any node within the network, no matter what route the information would have to travel. As long as there was some way to bring data from A to B it could be achieved by the network, even if the information had to take a detour. This kind of flexible delivery was made possible by using a packet-switching system instead of the old line-switching system to transfer the data. In line-switching, the transfer of data is achieved by using a direct line between the communication partners. This line has to be established explicitly before the transfer of data. If one of the switching points breaks down, the transmission cannot be completed. Packet-switching, on the other hand, converts the data into small standardized packages that are then sent individually through the network, taking different routes. Each package contains address information that it uses to find the correct destination. At their destination, the packages are put together to again represent the initial message.

The idea of a centreless, packet-switching network was first put to work in the form of the military-funded ARPANET. The name comes from the US Department of Defense's Advanced Research Projects Agency (ARPA). In December 1969, this forerunner of today's Internet connected four universities and research institutions along the west coast of the United States.

Already in the early years of the Internet, one of the problems its developers faced was the need to connect very different types of computers. They needed a strategy to allow packet-switched communication, regardless of the hardware used at the sites involved. The solution consisted of the TCP/IP communications protocols. As mentioned above, protocols generally contain agreements on how to organize the transmission of data in a computer network. TCP/IP uses detailed modes of procedure that permit communication within a heterogeneous network. The development of TCP/IP began in 1976, although the protocols did not come into full use until 1983.

The Internet was initially a network used only by the military and by educational and research institutions. By the end of the 1980s, however, it had also become available for commercial and private users, not only in the United States but all over the world.

How to connect to the Internet

In order to access Internet services, the user's computer must be connected to the Internet. Computers that are part of a network, for example a company's or university's local area network (LAN), fulfil this requirement if their local network is connected to the Internet itself. This kind of Internet connection is a permanent one. The costs are usually carried by the institution running the local network.

If you do not have access to a permanent connection, you will have to connect to the Internet by using your phone lines to set up a temporary connection. The physical connection consists of your PC, a modem or ISDN adapter and the analogue or digital phone lines. However, you also need an Internet Service Provider (ISP) that is already part of the Internet and which will allow you to use its computer as a gateway to the Internet. There are a multitude of ISPs. The major international online services – America Online (AOL), CompuServe, or Germany's T-Online – also act as ISPs. The costs for the phone connection and the ISP's additional service charges have to be paid by the individual user.

Internet services

The computers and transmission channels that make up the physical infrastructure of the Internet allow for a variety of networked activities or services. The services available can be categorized as follows:

Communication services
- E-mail
- Mailing Lists
- Usenet Newsgroups
- Internet Relay Chat (IRC).

Information services
- worldwide web (WWW)
- Telnet
- File Transfer Protocol (FTP)
- Gopher, Veronica
- Archie
- Wide Area Information Service (WAIS).

Communication services

The Internet's physical infrastructure allows for a variety of communication forms. Here we will consider each of them with respect to their relevance for the translation process.

E-mail
Sending and receiving electronic mail (e-mail) is the most widely used Internet service. For translators it is a very useful tool for exchanging data with clients or for communicating with clients and colleagues (see Chapter 2).

Mailing lists
Mailing lists are virtual discussion circles where the participants exchange ideas on any given subject in the form of e-mails. A mailing list is identified by a single name. When an e-mail message is sent to the mailing list name, it is automatically forwarded to all the addresses that have subscribed to the list. That way you can send your e-mail to a great number of people by simply sending it to the mailing list address. Further, you will automatically receive all mails sent by other subscribers to the list. This kind of broadcasting or one-to-many communication is useful if you want to stay up to date with the latest trends in a specific field or you want to distribute questions to a number of people interested in the same field as you. For translators it can be an efficient way to contact experts in various fields or to get help with terminology issues.

A major linguistically oriented mailing list is the Linguist List. In order to become a participant you need to send an e-mail to the list address, which is listserv@listserv.linguist.org. Leave the reference line blank, and type 'subscribe [Your Name]' in the mail body. The Linguist List is also available through the WWW at http://linguistlist.org/.

A translation-related mailing list is Lantra-L. To subscribe to the list, send a mail to listserv@segate.sunet.se (no reference line, text: Sub Lantra-L [Your Name]). Lantra-L is accessible through the WWW as well (http://segate.sunet. se/archives/LANTRA-L.html or http://www.geocities.com/Athens/7110/ lantra.htm).

Newsgroups

Like mailing lists, newsgroups are discussion and information platforms. They are also called online conferences. A message (news) sent to a newsgroup becomes available to a large number of people. However, the messages sent to a newsgroup are not always automatically forwarded to each individual in a mailing list, but are posted on an electronic bulletin board, for everyone entering the newsgroup to see.

Internet Relay Chat

Internet Relay Chat (IRC), named after the protocol on which it is based, also makes live online discussion between a large number of participants possible. The 'talking' (chatting) is done by typing your comments on the keyboard. The symbols you enter automatically appear on the discussion screen. In order to become an IRC discussant, you need an IRC client and Internet access. The IRC client is a program that runs on your computer and sends and receives messages to and from an IRC server. Unlike the asynchronous discussion made possible by mailing lists and newsgroups, IRC makes direct and interactive live discussion possible. However, since the members of the discussion group are not identifiable (they are identifiable in newsgroups), the validity and reliability of the discussion contributions is not clearly verifiable.

Information services

Information can be sought on the Internet in various ways. What they all have in common is the fact that data are provided by a host computer, a server. The data are retrieved with the help of a client program and the information is transmitted in the form of files. Most of these services have already been incorporated into the worldwide web, which has thus become a multifunctional and comprehensive information service.

Telnet

Telnet is a terminal emulation program, which means that it allows you to access a larger computer (e.g. a mainframe) with a PC by 'posing' as a terminal connected to that computer. It is especially designed for networks that, like the Internet, are based on TCP/IP. Telnet allows you to connect with remote computers, enabling you to enter commands and thus control the remote computer as if you were sitting directly in front of it. Access to remote computers is usually restricted by the use of login names and passwords. Many libraries still use the Telnet service to allow you access to their online catalogues. Some online databases are also available via Telnet.

File Transfer Protocol

The File Transfer Protocol (FTP) service is named after the protocol used to transfer files over the Internet (or any other TCP/IP-based network). It allows you to access special computers called FTP servers, from which you can download files to your own computer or upload files to the FTP server. FTP is often used to transfer program updates. Some translation clients now deliver source texts and background information via FTP. Glossaries can also be downloaded from FTP sites, the most popular being Microsoft's multilingual glossaries available at ftp://ftp.microsoft.com/developr/msdn/newup/glossary/.

FTP downloads are supported by most modern web browsers. Simply type the FTP address in the browser's address field and hit the Enter key.

Archie, Gopher and Veronica

Archie servers contain databases listing the contents of a multitude of FTP servers. This facilitates the search for FTP resources.

Gopher is an information system for organizing and displaying files on Internet servers. Developed at the University of Minnesota and named after the school's mascot, it enables you to browse the Internet resources displayed in a hierarchical list of files.

Veronica is a program that allows you to search global indices of resources stored in Gopher systems. A similar system is known as Jughead. With the advent of the WWW, Gopher has become outdated and more and more Gopher servers are being converted to websites for easier access.

Wide Area Information Search

Wide Area Information Search (WAIS, pronounced *ways*) lets you search document databases. The texts to be searched have to be tagged in a specific, WAIS-compatible format. Connection to a WAIS server is done in the form of a Telnet session (see below).

The worldwide web

The worldwide web (WWW) is the latest and definitely the most influential of the many Internet services available. It was developed by Tim Berners-Lee at the European Laboratory for Particle Physics in Geneva in the late 1980s. The WWW was the first graphical user interface for accessing the contents of the Internet. Before the WWW emerged, the information exchanged on the Internet was character-based, making it impossible, for example, to send graphics over the Internet. In addition to opening up the Internet to the use of multimedia applications, the WWW allowed for the linking of WWW resources by providing electronic links, so-called hyperlinks, between documents stored on WWW servers.

In order to access information stored on WWW servers, users need special programs or WWW clients. The clients are called 'browsers', the most popular being Netscape's Navigator and Microsoft's Internet Explorer. Modern browsers also offer features that let the user access other Internet services such as FTP or Telnet. In addition, mail clients such as Netscape's Messenger are integrated into browser software packages and enable users to send and receive electronic mail without having to open a separate e-mail program.

A client–server architecture

How do data from one of the computers on the Internet find their way onto my screen? The structure of the WWW is based on what is known as a 'client–server' principle. This means that one computer contains the information that a second computer wants to have. This second computer uses a 'client', in our case a web browser, to access the data stored on the WWW computer, i.e. the 'server'. The client submits a request to the server, asking it to transfer the data in the form of a file. This request takes the form of an Internet address, known as a URL (Uniform Resource Locator). You can enter the URL directly into the address field of your browser or you can send it by activating a hyperlink in a given document. The server then processes the request and carries it out. The browser receives the information, i.e. the file or files sent by the server, and displays the server's response on the screen. The files transferred between server and client on the worldwide web are written in a specific language called HTML, or HyperText Markup Language. This basically consists of plain ASCII text but contains mark-up information, called tags, that allow for a multitude of formatting and display options, including the ability to integrate hyperlinks in the document. Any text that contains hyperlinks is called a 'hypertext'. Hypertext documents are transferred via the Internet on the basis of a common set of communication rules, known as the HyperText Transfer Protocol (HTTP).

Let's see how the WWW works:

1. Start your browser (e.g. Netscape Navigator or MS Internet Explorer). Enter the following URL in the location or address field of your browser: http:// www.pcwebopedia.com/Networks/Ethernet/collision.html. Now hit Enter.
2. The client takes the URL that you entered and breaks it down into its individual components. Using HTTP it will try to display the file 'index.html' on your screen. The client knows that it will find the file named 'collision.html' in the subdirectory Ethernet, which itself can be found in the directory Networks on a server named www.pcwebopedia.com. The URL

components to the right of the top-level domain (.com) refer to the individual storage system of the server. The address scheme of URLs will be discussed in detail in Chapter 4.

3. The client transfers the URL to something called a DNS server. DNS stands for Domain Name Service, an Internet service that translates domain names into IP (Internet Protocol) addresses. While the computers that make up the Internet use numeric IP addresses to contact each other, the user works with alphabetic domain names, because they are easier to remember. So every time you use a domain name, a DNS service must translate the name into the corresponding IP address. The DNS server browses its tables with matching URL and IP addresses and produces the numeric IP address of the server that you have requested the information from.

4. Now, using HTTP, the browser takes the IP address provided by the DNS server to contact the WWW server. At this stage, all the computers – the client and the server – do is 'shake hands', as it is called, and introduce themselves. The client lets the server know that it would like to have some information, and in return the server asks what kind of information the client would like to receive. Taking the information contained in the URL that you entered, the client specifies its request for the file 'collision.html' stored in the subdirectory Ethernet in the directory Networks.

5. Look at the status bar of your browser window (at the bottom of the screen) to observe what is happening. You can see that the client is contacting the server.

6. Once the server has received this request it looks for the file. If the file cannot be found (it may have been deleted, renamed or moved to a different location) an error message indicating the reason for the error is displayed.

7. If the file exists, the server starts to transfer it. In the status line you can see the progress of the data transfer. The browser receives the file in HTML format, decodes it and displays it on the screen. If the HTML file contains additional files, for example an embedded image, the browser contacts the server again and requests the transfer of the specific graphic file. The server sends the file (along with any additional files that form part of the initially requested HTML file) and composes the document on your screen.

8. Once the transfer is completed, the connection between client and server is terminated.

Note: Any transfer from the server to the client and vice versa can be interrupted by clicking the Stop symbol in your browser's toolbar.

Naming scheme

Resources are easily accessed on the WWW because the system is based on a uniform naming scheme. In fact, deducing Internet addresses from the name of an organization can become an efficient search strategy: if you know how URLs are structured, they can tell you more or less where you are going. As we have seen, clients use URLs to find information on web servers. If you enter www.yahoo.com in your web browser, you enter the URL of Yahoo's web server.

How URLs are organized

In order to discover how a URL is structured, take a look at the following address: http://www.lib.harvard.edu. Note that it does not matter if the URL is in capitals. Capitalization only matters for the parts of an address that follow the top-level domain and that refer to a specific directory or file. That part is separated from the top-level domain by a forward slash (/).

You have probably already guessed that this URL belongs to the website of Harvard University's main library. Look at the URL, starting from the end. The last part – edu – is called a top-level domain (TLD). The other component parts of the URL are called sub-domains. The letters 'edu' stand for 'education' and signify that this URL belongs to an educational institution in the United States (rules for naming top-level domains vary between the United States and the rest of the world).

The component 'harvard' tells you the name of the institution to which you want to pay a virtual visit, in this case Harvard University in Cambridge, Massachusetts. 'Lib' designates the part of the institution (for example, a department or group) that you are specifically interested in (in this case the library system of Harvard University). If you leave out the library sub-domain, you will get to Harvard's general homepage (http://www.harvard.edu).

The first part of the URL – http:// – designates the communications protocol to be used to transfer the information you have requested. HTTP is the standard protocol for transferring HTML documents on the Internet.

Knowing the basics of a URL structure and being a little creative with abbreviations lets you guess many URLs. Let's try to guess the URLs of some American universities.

- Yale: www.yale.edu (not hard!)
- University of California at Los Angeles (think of abbreviations, since a domain name cannot have more than 22 characters). This should give us: http://www.ucla.edu
- what about the University of California at Berkeley? No, not http://www.ucb.edu; nice try. It is http://www.berkeley.edu
- as a last test, how about San Francisco State University? http://www.sfsu.edu.

Top-level domains

As you can see, top-level domains are intended to help categorize Internet resources. That is why they are also called generic top-level domains (GTLDs). GTLDs can be quite helpful for users who want to know what kind of institution they are about to access.

As we have mentioned, the top-level domains of US-based institutions can differ from those in other parts of the world. Let's take a look at the US top-level domains and their meanings:

.com: Commercial institutions. Most companies (not only in the United States but increasingly all over the world) use this TLD. It is the most widely used TLD. Try www.microsoft.com, www.netscape.com, www.aol.com or in the case of non-US companies, www.sap.com, www.nokia.com or www.bt.com.

.mil: This is the domain used for websites belonging to the US military (www.af.mil for the US Air Force or www.ja.hq.af.mil for the US Air Force's Judge Advocate General).

.net: This GTLD designates companies or organizations that act as network providers or have to do with the administration of networks (e.g. www.arin.net, the American Registry for Internet Numbers, which is responsible for the management of Internet addresses in the United States and assigned territories).

.edu: Originally designed to designate the websites of all educational entities in the United States (universities, colleges, schools, educational service organizations, etc.), registrations have been recently restricted to four-year colleges and universities. Schools and two-year colleges will be registered in the country domain US.

.gov: This TLD is reserved for agencies of the US Federal government such as the State Department (www.state.gov), the Senate (www.senate.gov) or the White House (www.whitehouse.gov). The Library of Congress, which offers enormous bibliographical information through its online catalogues, also carries this TLD (www.loc.gov).

.org: This TLD is used by organizations of various kinds, most notably international entities such as the United Nations (ww.un.org) or the World Bank (www.worldbank.org). Various other non-profit organizations are also registered under this TLD.

.int: This TLD is meant for organizations established by international agreements. Not many websites have this TLD, notable exceptions being NATO (www.nato.int), the European Union (http://europa.eu.int/) and the International Telecommunications Union (ITU) (www.itu.int), which among other things offers a multilingual terminology database (Termite).

Country domains

In addition to the US-specific domains, there are hundreds of country domains and sub-domains used to describe a website's origin. Country domains normally use the codes assigned by the International Standardization Organization (ISO). The codes usually consist of the first two letters of the country's original name, e.g. IT for Italy (Italia), ES for Spain (España), DE for Germany (Deutschland). A list of all country codes is available at http://www.ics.uci.edu/ pub/websoft/wwwstat/country-codes.txt (from the University of California at Irvine). Within each country domain, several sub-domains are used to indicate the kind of institution that is posting the information. Universities in Britain, for example, have the following URL structure: www.universityname.ac.uk, where .ac stands for academia. The URL of Oxford is thus www.oxford.ac.uk. Spanish universities are sometimes marked by the letter U directly followed by the city name, e.g. www.uvigo.es, or use abbreviated forms of their official name, such as www.uc3m.es (Universidad Carlos III de Madrid). German universities have addresses like www.uni-heidelberg.de or www.uni-goettingen.de. German polytechnics (*Fachhochschulen*) can be found by combining the abbreviation FH (for *Fachhochschule*) with the name of the location, e.g. www.fh-magdeburg.de. In cities with various universities, proper names or their abbreviations are often used as part of the URL. Since university servers are often of valuable help to translators searching for background information or terminology resources, awareness of their URL schemes can make your online research much more productive.

Homepages, webpages and websites

Every document that you transfer from a web server to display on your screen consists of one or several files (e.g. a text document with embedded graphic files). In general, every single document displayed on your screen is called a webpage. A combination of single webpages that are thematically and physically linked together is referred to as a website (so the website of a company or organization can be made up of various webpages). The entrance gate to a website is usually called a homepage. A homepage serves as the starting point for navigation through a website. It can be considered the first level of a hierarchical website structure.

Some webpages are composed of several sections, called frames. This feature enables the author of a webpage to divide up the display area in order to structure the content. The contents of each frame come from a different file (or webpage).

Web browsers and their most important features

Web browsers are the client applications that allow you to access the numerous Internet services available. They offer a variety of features. Here we will just look at those that you are most likely to use when searching for information. Most of these features can be activated by clicking on the respective symbols in the tool bar of your browser. Figure 11 shows the title, menu, tool and address bars of Netscape's Navigator.

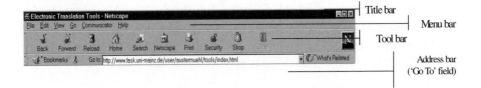

Figure 11. Using Netscape's features

- *Entering URLs* Just enter the URL of the site or page you want to access in the Go To field and hit the Enter key. The addresses you enter in this field are saved. The list of previously entered URLs can be seen by clicking on the down arrow at the end of the Go To field. In the list that appears, you can select the URL you want to visit again by just clicking on it.
- *Navigating between webpages that you have already accessed* Using the Back and Forward arrows in the tool bar you can quickly access the documents that you have most recently opened. These documents are stored in a History list, which you can look at by opening the Go menu.
- *Saving and opening webpages* If you want to save the contents of a document, open the File menu and click Save As (or Save Frames in the case of a webpage containing frames). Then select a location and name for the file. You can also open locally stored files by clicking File/Open Page/ Choose File.
- *Printing a document* To print a web document displayed on the screen, simply click the Print symbol in the tool bar. Be careful with large documents; you might want to check how long the document is first (File/Print Preview) and/or only print out a few pages at a time.
- *Bookmarking a webpage* A bookmark allows you to save the URLs of a webpage that you intend to visit more often. Simply click on Bookmarks in the address bar, and then click Add Bookmark to store the title and URL of the document currently displayed. You can also use the shortcut Ctrl+D to bookmark a document. The bookmark feature is a very powerful instrument when organizing your URLs, and you should learn how to work with bookmarks early on.
- *Finding text in a webpage* When looking for certain words or expressions in a large document, the search function provided by the browser is very handy. By choosing Edit/Find in Page (Shortcut: Ctrl+F), you can activate this feature (which is almost the same as the one you use in word-processing). Enter the string you are looking for and click on Find.
- *Stopping data transfer* If you want to stop the transfer of a file, simply click on the Stop symbol in the tool bar.
- *Selecting a start page* By clicking on the Home symbol in the tool bar, the browser opens a predetermined document. This home or start page for your

browser can be customized. Click on Edit/Preferences/Navigator. In the Homepage section you can determine which document the browser should open when it starts. The document can be a document stored on a web server or it can be a locally stored file (e.g. your bookmark file).

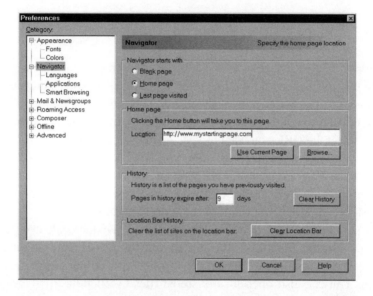

Figure 12. Customizing your browser

Tasks

✓ What is a communications protocol?
✓ Define the role of TCP/IP.
✓ What does FTP stand for?
✓ What kind of Internet services do you know?
✓ What is the difference between the worldwide web and the Internet?
✓ What is the difference between a website and a webpage?
✓ What is a frame?
✓ What TLDs do you know?
✓ What is the URL of your university's homepage?
✓ Find the website of the World Bank; use your web browser to bookmark it.

Further reading and Internet links

Berners-Lee, T., M. Fischetti, M. Dertouzos (1999) *Weaving the Web: The Original Design and Ultimate Destiny of the World Wide Web by its Inventor*, San Francisco: Harper.
Dyson, E. (1998) *Release 2.1: A Design for Living in the Digital Age*, New York:

Broadway Books.

Gralla, P. et al. (1999) *How the Internet Works : Millennium Edition*, Indianapolis: Que.

Kehoe, B.P. (1992): *Zen and the Art of the Internet. A Beginner's Guide to the Internet*, First Edition, January 1992, http://www.cs.indiana.edu/docproject/zen/zen-1.0_toc.html (Nov. 27, 2000).

Yahoo's directory of beginner's guides to the WWW: http://dir.yahoo.com/Computers_and_Internet/Internet/World_Wide_Web/Beginner_s_Guides/ (Nov. 27, 2000).

4. Searching the web

Finding data on the worldwide web is no problem at all. But finding *reliable information* is a rather difficult task. And finding the information you really need can be very time-consuming and often frustrating.

To avoid getting lost in cyberspace, you need a few search strategies. This is especially true for the multidisciplinary information needs of translators. At the time of writing, there are about 1 billion WWW documents available, and to find the one document that might contain the answer to your query could be like looking for the proverbial needle in a haystack. You may have heard that 'search engines' are the answer to all your prayers. These are programs accessible on the web that contain large indexes of millions of websites. However, according to a study published in *Nature* magazine (Chiu 1999:111), even the most popular and most powerful search engines such as Northern Light (http://www.northernlight.com), Hotbot (http://hotbot.lycos.com) or AltaVista (http://www.altavista.com) each only cover up to 16 percent of the web's contents. Combined, the largest search engines still miss out on half of the available documents. Subject trees like Yahoo (http://www.yahoo.com), which enable the user to browse through information categorized by subjects, cover even less of the information available.

What is required for the heterogeneous information needs of translators is a multi-level approach to Internet research, a top-down approach comprising three interconnected strategies:

- institutional search
- thematic search
- keyword search.

These strategies will be explained in detail in the following chapters. But they must first be based on a thorough evaluation of the quality of the various websites to be visited.

Web search strategies 1 – institutional search via URLs

Before you start surfing the web for translation-related information, you should always ask yourself a few basic questions: What kind of information do I need? What might be a reliable source for this kind of information? Whom do I trust? Since documents on the WWW can contain all kinds of false and unreliable data, identifying the information providers you can trust is an important step towards ensuring the quality of the information you obtain. Comparing the virtual world with the real one can sometimes help you identify trustworthy content suppliers.

Newspapers online

Let us start with a few simple examples. Let's say you want to check the latest
football scores (I am talking about real, i.e. European, football here). Where do
you usually get them on Sunday or Monday mornings? Most likely in the papers, in the sports sections (or on the front page). This 'research approach' will
also work in cyberspace. Numerous newspapers have their own websites. For
the football example, take one of the newspapers you know – let's say *El País*
for Spain. What is its address? You can more or less guess it by using the standard URL structure http://www.institutionname.topleveldomain. The name of
the institution in this case is El País (note: URLs are case-insensitive and accents are left out); the TLD for Spain is ES; so the URL of *El País* is www.
elpais.es. Try to find the football results either by checking the front page or by
accessing the sports section (Deportes).

Try to find some other newspapers. How about Italy's *La Repubblica*,
France's *Le Figaro*, *The Guardian* in the UK, Germany's *Süddeutsche Zeitung*?
The archives of online newspapers provide a tremendous pool of translation-
related information. They will be dealt with in greater detail in Chapter 5.

If you are interested in American football scores, let's say the National Football League (NFL), you can of course visit the websites of American newspapers
or news services. Try http://www.washingtonpost.com (remember, the most
common top-level domain in the US is com for commercial sites). You might
try the *Los Angeles Times* for more detailed West Coast coverage http://
www.latimes.com, or http://www.cleveland.com (*Cleveland Plain Dealer*) if
you happen to be a Browns fan. You could also go to the website of the organization that is most likely to be a very reliable expert on American football. In
this case it is the NFL itself. What URL would they have, http://www.nfl.org?
Are you sure? Look at the millions of dollars these clubs and players make . . .
Okay, now you've got it: the URL is http://www.nfl.com.

International organizations

Other valuable web resources are the sites of international organizations. Most
of them can be found using the URL search method. Most of these sites are
great sources of information for translators, especially when it comes to parallel
texts that offer both background and support for text production. Many of them
also provide glossaries or even databases with the terminology of their respective fields. Again, ask yourself first: What kind of information do I need? Who
might have it? Who is reliable?

Let's go through a few scenarios. We'll start with the easy ones: the United
Nations and its institutions. The UN's website can be found at http://www.un.org;
UNESCO is at http://www.unesco.org, despite the fact that it is located in Paris.

UNICEF's URL is ...? Well, try for yourself. And how about NATO: http://www.nato.org? No, sorry. As I said earlier, NATO's website is one of the few that carries the ominous .int top level domain. You will find it at http://www.nato.int.

Now, where would you look for texts on refugees, on global energy politics, on food programmes? How do you find the English, Spanish, French texts of a specific UN resolution? Is there a French and English glossary on conservation?

Since these large organizations usually offer a large amount of information (and thus sometimes have heavily loaded homepages), you should look for links leading directly to lists of documents or to document databases, or perhaps links that enable you to search the contents of the website. If you are looking for Spanish versions of UN resolutions, you might start your quest at the UN's international website at http://www.un.org. By clicking on the Spanish link, you change to the Spanish-language website of the UN. From there, you can click on 'Documentos y mapas', where you will find, amongst other things, documents from the Security Council, including a list of resolutions sorted chronologically.

Another example: Let's say you are translating a text on water pollution. The UN's environmental programme (http://www.unep.org) will probably have some information on the subject. The same goes for the World Bank, whose website (http://www.worldbank.org) offers a variety of information, including parallel texts and numerous glossaries.

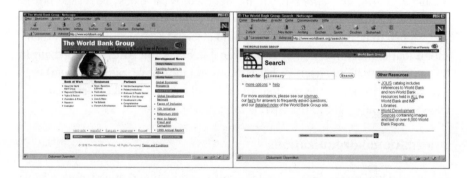

Figure 13. Searching the website of the World Bank

As you can see in Figure 13, the homepage of the World Bank offers a variety of choices. To see what kinds of glossaries the World Bank has, you can use the search function (simply click on the Search button in the lower left-hand corner), and then search for the term 'Glossary'. All the documents in the website that contain the term 'glossary' will be listed in the results document. By then clicking on the hyperlinked name of the document, you can see its contents on the screen. In this case, click on the Glossary Table to list information of a glossary of fish terms.

Another example: Let's assume you are translating a medical text from English into Italian and you need to find documents that help you understand how medical texts are written in Italian. Using your knowledge about the real world, try to find the websites of an Italian institution known for its expertise in the field of medicine.

Admittedly, the institutional approach to web searching might lead you to very general information at the beginning. Once you have found the homepage of an institution that you think might provide valuable information, you need to find a way to search the contents of that institution's website more thoroughly. To do so, look for features and buttons like Search, Documents, Databases, Press or Glossaries, which serve as indicators for more detailed information.

Web search strategies 2 – thematic search via subject trees

Subject trees, or catalogues, are web-based search utilities that group the available information into categories. Users can thus search for information by selecting the thematic category (and sub-category) they are interested in. The best-known and most powerful subject tree is Yahoo.

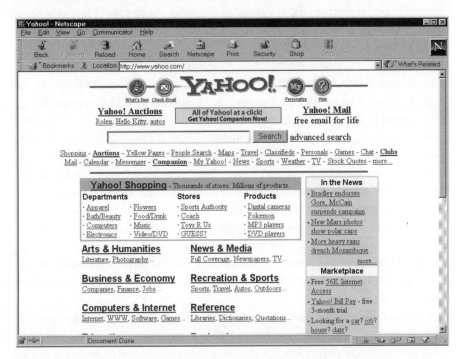

Figure 14. Yahoo's international homepage

Unlike search engines that are based on automatically generated indices of websites and pages, Yahoo relies on humans to find information and to catego- rize it. Since this is a rather time-consuming activity, the Yahoo information base comprises far fewer websites than those of search engines. However, we shall see that Yahoo co-operates with search engines to overcome this deficit.

The basic strategy when working with subject trees is to find a category and/or sub-category that might fit your information need. If you are looking for a specific newspaper or magazine, you would start with the main category News & Media, and then check the sub-categories Newspapers or Magazines. If you want to see what kind of dictionaries are available online, you start with References and then go to Dictionaries. As you can see from Figure 14, Ya- hoo's homepage lists not only the main (or top-level) categories, but gives you a glance at some of the sub-categories. Remember, however, that the sub- categories shown here are only a few of the many available. And, of course, each sub-category can contain further subcategories, and so on. When you per- form your search within a Yahoo sub-category, you can indicate whether the search should be conducted only in that sub-category or across the entire web.

In addition to its international website, Yahoo offers localized versions of its subject tree in many languages (see the bottom of the international homepage at http://www.yahoo.com for details). Not only are these sites presented in vari- ous languages but the information and websites belonging to the individual categories are taken from the region of the language presented. For example, a Spanish version of Yahoo can be found at http://es.yahoo.com (http://www. yahoo.es also works).

Try to find a Spanish introduction to the Integrated Services Digital Net- work (ISDN, RDSI in Spanish) to be used as a source of terminology for an English–Spanish translation of a website for a British telecom company. Using subject trees is a permanent decision-making process. First, you have to decide what category the subject ISDN belongs to. Since ISDN is a telecommunica- tions network based on digital data transmission, you might either start with Ciencia y tecnología (Science and Technology) or with Internet y ordenadores (Internet and Computers). Both routes will eventually take you to the same docu- ments, since the editors often put a website into various sub-categories as well as listing a given sub-category in various superordinated categories. Click on Internet y ordenadores to see the list of sub-categories. Here you will also find the entry Telecomunicaciones. As you can see from Figure 15, the entry is fol- lowed by the @-sign, which indicates that the sub-category can be found in other categories as well.

Click on Telecomunicaciones to see what this sub-category has to offer. As you can see in the Location field of your browser in the upper part of the Telecomuniciones page (Figure 16), this category actually belongs to the top-level category Ciencia y tecnología and is stored in the sub-categories

Ingeniería and Ingeniería eléctrica. Nevertheless, you managed to reach your goal, where the reward for your search is a link to an 'Introducción a la RDSI'. Click on the link to find an elaborate document on the subject, which you can use as a resource for your translation project.

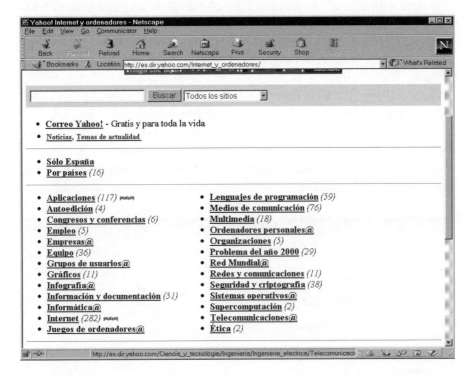

Figure 15. The sub-category Internet y ordenadores in Yahoo's Spanish site

In addition to accessing websites through the subject categories, Yahoo lets the user look for keywords in its collection of categories, websites and webpages. When you do this, you can combine the flexibility of a search engine with the thematic structure of a subject tree.

The keyword search can be activated from the Yahoo homepage (both on the international site as well as on the national ones) by simply typing one or more words into the search field and then clicking on the Search or, in this case, Buscar button.

The results of the search are grouped into four areas, represented in the bar in the upper part of the results page:

Categories (Categorías) This refers to the names of categories and sub-categories in Yahoo that match the keyword you entered. In this case (RDSI) there are no categories or sub-categories in Yahoo's Spanish site that match the keyword (so the word Categorías is displayed with a light grey background, which indicates that no matches were found). Instead, websites (sitios web) are offered as the search results (marked blue).

Websites (Sitios web) This group of documents refers to sites that have been registered with Yahoo, i.e. sites that have already been allocated to one of Yahoo's categories. In this case, the search result provides the title of the website, a short description of it, and the category it belongs to. By clicking on the title of the document of interest, the user can call that page up on the screen.

Webpages (Páginas web) If Yahoo is unable to find any categories of sites within its own catalogue, it passes the user's inquiry along to a search engine which in turn processes the query and displays those documents contained in its own index. Even if Yahoo finds matching categories or websites, you can activate the search for more matching webpages by clicking on the entry 'Web Pages' in the bar of the results page.

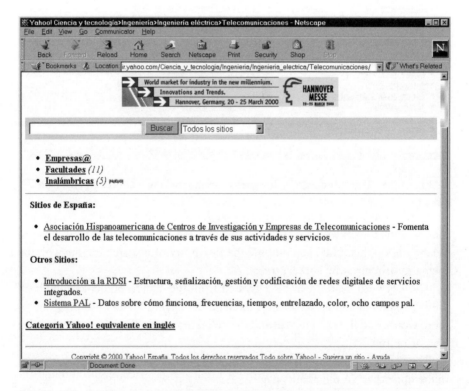

Figure 16. The sub-category Telecomunicaciones

Related News (Noticias): This fourth group of results refers to news articles from a variety of sources, including Associated Press (AP) and Reuters, which contain the keyword you searched for.

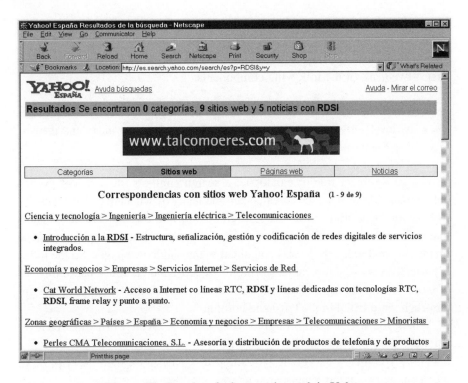

Figure 17. Results of a keyword search in Yahoo

If you enter more than one keyword, you can combine these words in a number of ways (e.g. using Boolean operators, see below).

Web search strategies 3 – word search via search engines

The institutional ('URL guessing') and thematic (subject tree) approaches to finding information are very efficient at identifying a way through the plethora of information that is available; they are also very helpful in finding reliable sources. However, they are not the right tools for a comprehensive search of the countless webpages available. Indeed, at present no search tool would be able to list all the information contained in all the documents. Yet search engines such as AltaVista, Hotbot or Northern Light let the user search through the contents of several hundred million websites at a time. The results are usually quite numerous as well. AltaVista, for example, returns more than 1.7 million documents containing the search word ISDN, many more than you could expect from Yahoo.

How search engines work

Search engines do not use categories showing the origin of the webpages. They basically consist of the following components:

- a large index of words contained in web documents;
- retrieval software that lets you search for words in the index and then displays the matching documents on the screen.

Unlike a subject tree or catalogue, a search engine's index is not put together manually; instead, it is created automatically by what are called 'spiders', 'robots' or 'web crawlers'. These programs are like digital vacuum cleaners that visit a given website, record the URLs of the individual webpages making up the site, and index the words contained in the single webpages. So the index is basically a two-column table, storing in the left-hand column a list of billions of words and in the right-hand column the addresses of the webpages that contain each word listed in the left-hand column.

When you use a search engine to look for a given word, the retrieval software goes through the list of words, registering any entry or occurrence matching your query and giving you the title, URL, and a short description of the document containing the search word.

The searches conducted using search engines are based on words or characters. The machine looks for a string of characters listed in the index that matches the string of characters of your search query. The searches are case-insensitive, and diacritical symbols (e.g. accents) are ignored, as are any special characters (like ñ, æ, ß, etc.). Since the search is merely a process of comparing characters, there is no semantic differentiation. So if you are looking for a gift for your father-in-law, you should bear in mind that your search might come across some German websites talking about *Gift*, which means 'poison' and which will probably not be well received as a birthday present.

The syntax of search engines

Since search engines rely on the indexed content of hundreds of millions of webpages, they tend to deliver a multitude of documents as a result of a search query. For example, if you use Hotbot to search for the term 'dictionary' you will be presented with well over 1 million 'hits', i.e. documents matching your search word. To reduce the number of possible hits, you will want to enter not just one but several keywords that describe the nature of your query more precisely. Search engines let you combine numerous keywords in various ways. The way this combination is implemented depends on the individual search engine and its 'search syntax'.

Combining keywords is usually done using Boolean operators (AND, OR, NOT) and sometimes also by using proximity operators (NEAR, ADJ, etc.).

Boolean operators

The Boolean (or logical) operators AND, OR and NOT are offered by all search engines. Combining two or more keywords using the AND operator tells the search engine to look for documents that contain all the keywords entered, i.e. entering 'dictionary AND Spanish', will bring back documents that contain both terms. Yet this does not necessarily mean that the documents displayed all contain information on Spanish dictionaries. In some search engines the AND operator can be represented by a plus (or inclusion) sign directly preceding the keyword ('+dictionary +Spanish') or by the option 'all the words' that can usually be selected using a drop-down field.

The AND operator helps reduce the number of hits by using keywords as filter criteria. On the other hand, the OR operator ('any of the words') will enhance the number of hits. OR combinations are useful when the number of results is too small or if you want your search to include (quasi) synonyms (e.g. dictionary OR glossary) or foreign-language equivalents (e.g. dictionary OR diccionario OR dictionnaire).

The NOT operator represents an exclusion command, meaning that you do not want to display any documents that contain the excluded word or words. The NOT operator is often represented by a minus sign (e.g. dictionary -print).

Boolean operators can be combined in what is known as a Boolean phrase (e.g. dictionary AND Spanish OR Italian NOT English).

Proximity operators

Although Boolean operators are quite helpful in narrowing down or – in the case of the OR operator – expanding a search, they are often not precise enough, especially since they do not allow you to specify the distance between the search words that you enter. The use of another set of operators is thus sometimes necessary. The most frequent application of proximity operators is a phrase search. This kind of query searches only for the words you entered, in exactly the order you entered them. In many search engines, the phrase search is activated by enclosing the search words in quotes. For example, looking for 'Spanish dictionary' would result in a hit list containing documents containing exactly this phrase (and not 'dictionary, Spanish' or 'dictionary of Spanish'). Some search engines also offer the operators ADJ (for adjacent) or FOL-LOWED BY to enable a phrase search. Others let you use the operator NEAR BY, which means that the words combined occur within a short distance of each other, although the definition óf 'short distance' can vary from search engine to search engine, ranging from anywhere between two words and 100 characters. Proximity and Boolean operators can also be combined (e.g. 'Spanish dictionary' AND telecommunications NOT computers).

Advanced searching

In addition to a basic search, many search engines offer more sophisticated search options, often referred to as advanced or power searching. Using the example of Hotbot's advanced search feature, here we will demonstrate the additional advantages offered by this kind of search. Start the search feature by selecting the Advanced Search button on Hotbot's homepage (http://hotbot.lycos.com).

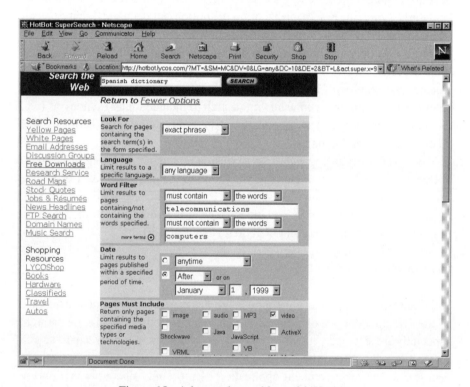

Figure 18. Advanced searching with Hotbot

One advantage of the advanced search is its clear structure. You work your way from the top to the bottom, starting by entering the keyword or words that are at the centre of your query in the line Search the Web. In the section Look For you can determine how you want various keywords to be connected. In addition to the operators AND (all the words), OR (any of the words), and the Boolean and proximity options mentioned above, you can also have the engine look for occurrences of the keywords entered in the title or URL of a webpage.

Searching for persons is also possible by selecting the Person option.

Once you have entered the keywords, Hotbot lets you specify your search in a variety of ways, all of them designed to reduce the number of documents to be searched by filtering out those that do not meet certain criteria.

Using the Language options you can have Hotbot search only in documents that have been marked as being presented in a specific language. In HTML this is done by integrating an invisible language-tag into the document's code. However, since this is not yet a standard procedure by web authors, filtering documents on the basis of their language-tag is not always recommended, since there is the danger that some documents might be overlooked.

The Word Filter is a very useful feature offered by Hotbot. Here you can enter additional words, phrases or names that a document must, should or must not contain. By default, two lines are offered in this section, but by clicking the More Terms button you can enhance these options to a total of five lines.

The Date section allows you to limit the number of documents to be searched to those published (or last updated) within a given period of time. You could then concentrate, for example, on only the most recent sites.

In the section Pages Must Include you can select various media types the document should contain. That way you can look for pages containing images or video sequences, for example, or, if you are interested in building your own corpus, text documents in WinWord or .pdf format.

Using Hotbot's Location/Domain options you can limit your search to documents from a specific type of organization or a specific region. By selecting .org, for example, Hotbot would look for your keywords only in documents coming from non-profit organizations. Entering '.it' would restrict the search to Italian sites.

As mentioned earlier, websites are usually composed of numerous individual webpages. A website can thus sometimes be a rather complex construction, with several levels of pages. Using the Page Depth option you can limit your search to a specific number of levels, e.g. only searching top-level pages (homepages).

The option Word Stemming allows for searches of grammatical variations of the keyword entered. If this option is activated, a search for 'development' would automatically include 'develop', 'developed', and so on.

As in the basic search, advanced searching lets you define how you want the results of your search to be displayed on the screen. You can limit the number of results to be shown at a time, and you can also select how much information should be displayed for each result (only URLs, short or long description). Choosing the long description allows you to decide whether you want to follow the link to a given site or not.

The advanced search features of other search engines work in a very similar way to that used by Hotbot. In any case, it might be a good idea to print out the online help for these search engines and to have the notes handy during the first stage of use.

There are numerous search engines available. The three mentioned here are just a few of the most powerful ones. The Website Search Engine Watch (http://www.searchenginewatch.com) constantly keeps track of the latest developments in the field; it is a very good starting point for finding out more. There you can also find information on regional search tools that focus on a specific geographic region, country or language.

Meta-search engines are tools accessible on the web that try to connect several independent search engines. This means that a search term entered in one of the meta-search engines (such as Dog Pile at http://www.dogpile.com or I-Sleuth at http://www.sleuth.com) will be forwarded for processing to a number of individual search engines. The results from these individual searches will be displayed together, while redundancies are deleted. Meta-search engines are basically a good idea. However, they are rather slow and do not offer as many options as individual search engines.

Ask Jeeves (http://www.askjeeves.com) is an online search tool that combines features of subject trees, search engines and meta-search engines with the ability to process queries submitted in natural languages (as opposed to the Boolean operators and proximity phrases mentioned above). Ask Jeeves also integrates your search terms into a predefined format (some are based on previous questions), thereby enabling you to specify your query by using the options offered by the 'butler' Jeeves.

Evaluating web documents

Due to the anarchic nature of the worldwide web, and since there is no co-ordinating or moderating organization involved in the online publishing of documents, you will find that many of the available webpages are lacking in accuracy, reliability and value. To ensure the quality of documents as resources and to avoid perpetuating incorrect data in your translations, you will have to develop your own quality-management strategy. This is especially true if you need to assess the quality of a document about a topic in which you are not an expert.

Your evaluation strategy should cover the following four aspects:

- information on the author of the document
- information on the document preparation process and its presentation
- meta-information and links to the document
- information on the accuracy and timeliness of the document's content.

The author's credentials

The validity of an online source depends very much on the credibility of its author. The author should be knowledgeable (i.e. an expert in the field they are writing about), reliable and, if you intend to use the document as a source of linguistic information, a native speaker of the language in which the document is written. Check a document for the following credentials:

- author's name and contact information (e-mail, snail mail, phone)
- biographical information on the author (nationality, working languages, education, training, publications, current job title and description)
- author's affiliation with organizations (academic, governmental, non-profit, corporate, etc.), including information on these organizations (use the URLs to find out about the organization posting the document)
- motivation for the publication of the document
- author's reputation among peers.

An anonymous or 'authorless' document should be accorded little credibility.

Document preparation process and presentation

The way a document's contents have been prepared and presented can also give you some information on its quality. Look for the following indicators:

- Is the document presented on an organizational website or an online journal? What is their reputation? Is peer review used?
- Was the information written only for the web, or was it taken from a source that went through an evaluation process (book, conference presentation, etc.)?
- What kinds of sources did the author use? Are there links to these sources, e.g. on a separate page? Does a bibliography exist?
- How is the information presented? Are larger documents split up into smaller sections? Are there any links to related websites? What is the quality of these websites?

Meta-information

Meta-information is information about information. In the case of web documents, meta-information refers both to reviews or summaries of the documents, and to references (links) from other web documents.

Reviews, commentaries or ratings can come from a variety of sources. Britannica Online, for example, offers hyperlinks to resources that are briefly described and rated. Yahoo's editors do the same thing with the sites gathered in their catalogue. Reviews can come from online journals; commentaries might be found in relevant newsgroups or on mailing lists.

Links to the documents can also help in evaluation. Using search engines you can find out how many webpages have published a hyperlink referring to the document in question. To do so, you enter 'link:' (e.g. in AltaVista) or

'LinkTo:' in the search field of the engine, followed by the URL of the document that you are evaluating. Make sure you assess the quality of the documents containing the link as well.

Accuracy and timeliness

Judging the accuracy and credibility of a document is very difficult and depends very much on the type of information presented. It is recommended that you check the factual data against reliable sources. For example, if you find a French term in a glossary on telecommunications provided by a British telecom company, and you are not sure whether you can use the term in your French translation, you might want to use the terminology database of the International Telecommunications Union, since this is the organization co-ordinating and actually defining global telecommunications standards. If you find a definition of any given term and you are not sure about the accuracy of the definition, you might use Britannica Online to double-check. If you read a nice phrase in an online document that you want to use in a translation, but you are not sure whether the author of the document is a native speaker, you might want to search for the phrase in the archives of *Newsweek* or the *Los Angeles Times* to verify its accuracy. This double-checking can be done online, but can also involve print sources or the consultation of domain experts.

In addition to letting you check the data in a document, there are further indicators of credibility (or lack thereof):

- timeliness of the information (last update, age of sources used, etc.)
- consistency of information (no contradictions, changing data, etc.)
- target group (was the document written for other professionals?)
- objectivity (bias, one-sided views, reasonable tone, etc.)
- spelling and grammatical errors.

Tasks

✓ What is the difference between a search engine and a subject tree?
✓ What is a Boolean operator?
✓ What is the advantage of using proximity operators?
✓ Use Search Engine Watch to find out which search engine has the largest index of web documents.
✓ Use Hotbot's advanced search option to find glossaries, dictionaries, etc. in your area of specialization (e.g. medicine, law, engineering).
✓ Use Yahoo to find glossaries, dictionaries, etc. in your area of specialization (e.g. medicine, law, engineering).
✓ What are the most important criteria for the evaluation of web documents?

Further reading and Internet links

Ackermann, E. and K. Hartman (1998) *The Information Specialist's Guide to Searching and Researching on the Internet and the World Wide Web*, Wilsonville, OR: Abf Content.

Chiu A.L.S., E. Sherry; X. Phung (1999) 'Just try to be specific', *Nature* 401/ 6749:111.

Harris, R. (1997) 'Evaluating Internet Research Sources', http://www.sccu.edu/ faculty/R_Harris/evalu8it.htm. Version Date: 17 Nov. 1997.

Hock, R. and P. Berinstein (1999) *The Extreme Searcher's Guide to Web Search Engines: A Handbook for the Serious Searcher*, Medford, N.J.: Information Today Inc.

Miller, S. (1998) *Searching the World Wide Web – An Introductory Curriculum for Using Search Engines*, Eugene, OR: International Society for Technology in Education.

AltaVista (search engine): http://www.altavista.com

Hotbot (search engine): http://hotbot.lycos.com

Northern Light (search engine): http://www.northernlight.com

Yahoo International (subject tree): http://www.yahoo.com

Ask Jeeves (natural language search): http://www.askjeeves.com

Dogpile (meta-search engine): http://www.dogpile.com

I-Sleuth (meta-search engine): http://www.sleuth.com

Search Engine Watch (search engine analysis): http://www.searchenginewatch.com

5. Translation resources on the worldwide web

The strategies for finding and evaluating information explained in the previous chapters will help you make the most of the resources to be found on the web. In this chapter we present a series of high-quality websites and explain how they can be incorporated into the translation process.

The retrieval of missing background knowledge plays an important role in the reception phase of the translation process. In order to understand the source text, it may be as necessary to use encyclopedias, knowledge databases or information retrieval systems as it can be to contact domain experts through newsgroups or mailing lists.

When searching for encyclopedic and linguistic information, translators need access to a multitude of resources. These resources can be offline or online. Offline resources (basically CD-ROMs) are explained in Chapter 6. Online resources are those available on the Internet, and they will be discussed here.

The following resources and sites will be featured in this chapter:

- online library catalogues, virtual bookstores
- general encyclopaedias: *Britannica online*
- specialized encyclopedias: *PC Webopedia*
- general monolingual dictionaries: *Merriam-Webster*
- general multilingual dictionaries: OneLook
- multilingual terminology databases: Termite, Eurodicautom
- newspaper and magazine archives: *ABC*, *Die Welt*, *Newsweek*.

Electronic bibliographical databases can be very helpful when looking for things such as introductory books on a given subject or when trying to find out whether a certain dictionary or encyclopedia already exists for the languages you are working in.

Using the Internet, a translator can conduct very efficient bibliographical searches, covering the whole world. In the following, we will use a bibliographical search for books in some of the world's most renowned national libraries. After that we will see how to use virtual online bookstores such as Amazon.com for bibliographical searches.

Accessing national libraries online

National libraries such as the British Library, the Bibliothèque Nationale de France, Die Deutsche Bibliothek or the Biblioteca Nacional de España offer exceptional amounts of bibliographical data. Most major libraries offer online access to their catalogues via OPACs (Open Access Online Catalogues). Here we shall see bibliographical searches in the online catalogues of the American Library of Congress and the Bibliothèque Nationale de France.

Accessing the Library of Congress online

The Library of the US Congress (LOC), physically located in Washington DC, is the largest library in the world. Its online catalogue or OPAC is available at http://catalog.loc.gov. Go to the site and click on the Guided Keyword button to start your search.

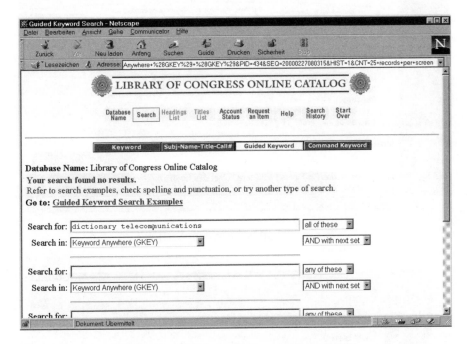

Figure 19. OPAC standard search form (LOC)

Fill in the search form. In the 'Search for' field, you enter the keyword you are looking for. The options in the 'Search in' field allow you to define the type of information you are looking for (e.g. the title of a book, author's name). The fields 'All of these' and 'Any of these' allow you to combine numerous search terms. Click on the Search button to run the query. The results of your search are then displayed in a hit list showing the titles of the books matching your search term and their years of publication. By clicking on an entry you can display a brief description of the publication.

The Bibliothèque Nationale de France

The Bibliothèque Nationale de France (BNF), the French national library, also

offers online access to its catalogue. The BNF's OPAC is available at http://
catalogue.bnf.fr/. Click on 'Connexion au catalogue' to start your online search.

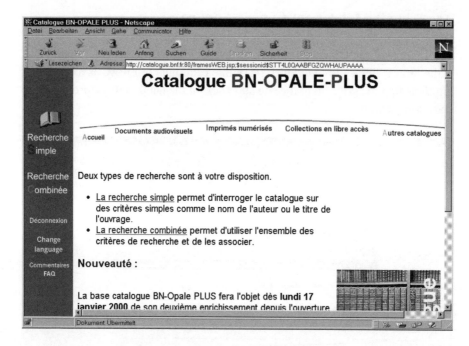

Figure 20. OPAC search types (BNF)

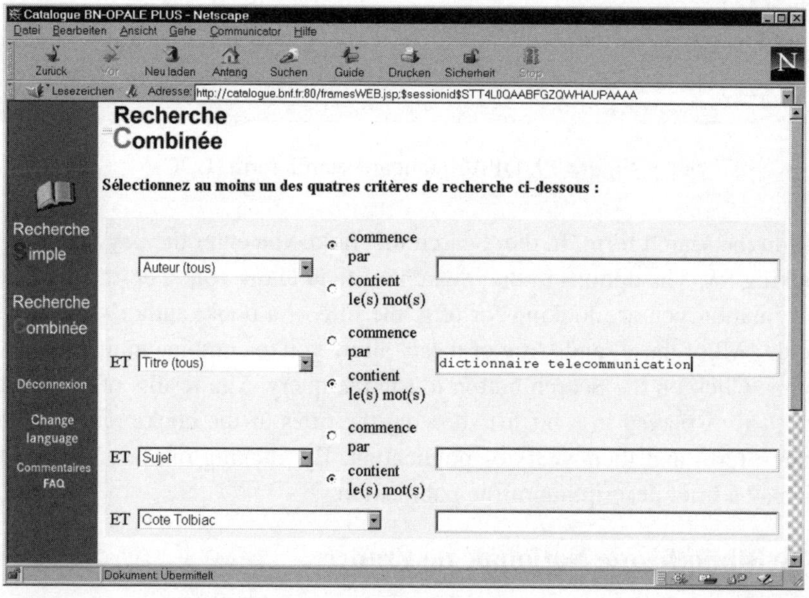

Figure 21. OPAC advanced search (BNF)

As you can see in Figure 20, the BNF also offers two search variants, 'La recherche simple' (basic search) or 'La recherche combinée' (advanced search). Try the latter.

Enter the keywords you are looking for. As you can see from Figure 21, you have several filter options to choose from. If you are looking for general works in a given discipline, it is usually most efficient to enter the search words in the title field and connect them with the Boolean AND operator. This option is the default setting for most search engines anyway.

Click on 'Lancer la recherche' to run your query. You will be given a list of catalogue entries that match your query. You can see more detailed information about a title by activating the check box to its right and then clicking on 'Voir les notices'. With this information you can then go to your local library or bookstore and ask for a hard copy of the book that you researched.

Browsing in virtual bookstores

Virtual bookstores such as Amazon (http://www.amazon.com) or Barnes & Noble (http://www.barnesandnoble.com) are also useful sources of bibliographical information. Indeed, their databases are larger than those of most universities.

Start your search in Amazon by clicking on the Books tab on Amazon's international homepage (Amazon also offers a German site at http://www.amazon.de and a UK site at http://www.amazon.co.uk).

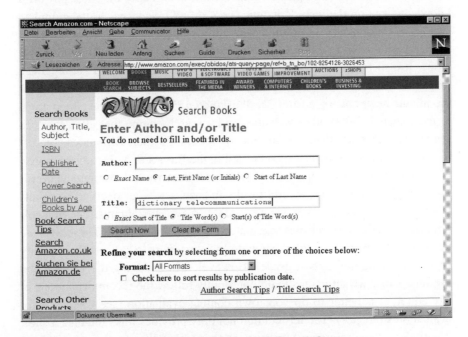

Figure 22. Amazon.com – Search form

Enter your search term – the name of the author or a keyword contained in the title of book – and click the Search Now button. The search feature allows you to look for exact as well as partial matches of search terms and bibliographic data. A list of matching books is then displayed. By clicking on the hyperlink title of the book or on the phrase 'Read more about this title' you can call up more detailed information (e.g. reviews or related books) on any of the books listed.

Virtual bookstores let you order books online, often at prices below the ones charged by physical bookstores. This can be especially useful for foreign-language books.

Encyclopedias and dictionaries

Encyclopedias and dictionaries have always been among translators' main tools, and the worldwide web offers a multitude of such reference works. Here we will demonstrate the power of these resources by looking at a few examples from the online version of the *Encyclopaedia Britannica*, the general Merriam-Webster Collegiate Dictionary, the meta-dictionary Onelook Dictionaries, and the specialized encyclopedic PC Webopedia.

Britannica.com – The mother of all encyclopedias goes online

The world's oldest and largest reference work is arguably the most powerful knowledge site on the web. Britannica.com offers free access to the complete articles of Britannica's 32-volume print edition, more than 72,000 articles and year-in-review texts in total. And the website is not restricted to Britannica data alone. It also features selected articles from more than 70 English-language magazines, among them *Newsweek*, *Time* and *The Economist*, as well as up-to-the-minute news coverage from *The Washington Post*. There is an edited guide to more than 125,000 other websites, and a search engine that allows you to search through more than 100 million webpages. Further, Britannica.com offers a bibliographical database connected to the Barnes & Noble online store.

When you use Britannica.com to search for the term 'telecommunications', for example, you will get several results in answer to your query. The results from the various databases and sources are displayed in columns. The first column provides links to websites that match the term you entered. These sites are taken from the Britannica Internet Guide and carry stars to indicate their quality (five stars being the highest grade). However, when judging the validity and usefulness of a website you should not blindly follow the recommendations of any editor; it is better to do your own content evaluation (see Chapter 4 for evaluation strategies). The left column not only provides links but also a short description of the referenced website, allowing you to assess its potential before you connect to it.

The second column contains articles taken from the *Encyclopaedia Britannica* that match your search term. By simply clicking on the hyperlinked title of the article, you can access the full article of the text. Each article offers a print view that enables you to print out the article.

In the third column you can find articles from a great number of magazines (*Newsweek, Discover, The Economist*, etc.) that have to do with the search term you entered. Column four, finally, represents entries from a book database. You can display the bibliographic data for the books related to your search, read more information on the content or author of the book, and can even order the book online through Britannica's partner Barnes & Noble.

The fastest way to search for any given term is to enter it in the search box on Britannica's homepage and then click on the Find button. You can also enter multiple words. If you do so, you can use the Boolean operators AND and OR and NOT and the proximity operator ADJ (for adjacent) to determine how you would like your search words to be combined. For example, if you enter 'mobile AND phone', you will only get articles that contain both search words. The query 'mobile ADJ phone' will only bring up articles containing the exact phrase 'mobile phone', that is, both search words have to appear in the article in exactly that order. The query 'mobile OR phone' is an 'any-search' and leads to a large number of results with articles that contain either the word 'mobile' or the word 'phone'. The operators have to be entered in upper case. Shortcuts can also be used instead of the full operators. A plus sign (+) replaces AND (e.g. mobile +phone), a minus sign (-) replaces NOT (e.g. mobile -phone), and putting the search words in quotes ("..."), represents a phrase or ADJ search (e.g. "mobile phone"). If you do not enter any operator or shortcut, Britannica will use the default setting OR to connect multiple search words. As you can see, Britannica's search feature works very much like major search engines such as Yahoo and Altavista.

In addition to the default simple search, there is an advanced search function. To access it, click on the tab 'Advanced search' on the Britannica homepage (Figure 23).

The advanced search offers the same operators that are available for the standard search. You can select the operators in the Contains box. The option 'the exact phrase' stands for the operator ADJ (or the shortcut " "). 'All of the Words' represents an AND (+) search, while 'any of the words' brings about an OR search. The option 'none of the words' excludes the words entered in this line, like NOT (-). You can also select which information source you would like to consult: all databases available (as in the standard search), only the magazines, only the Internet Guide or only all other webpages. You can also decide whether you only want the titles of the articles to be searched or whether to perform a full-text search of the entire documents. The latter is slower than searching through titles, but it is more extensive.

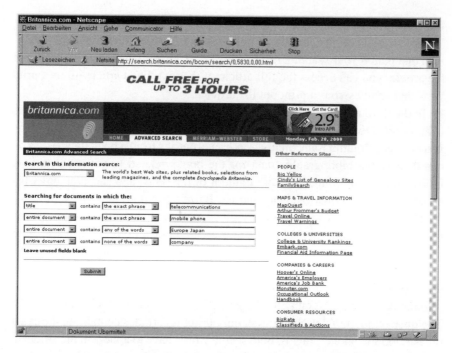

Figure 23. Britannica Online - Advanced search form

We will return to the full-text advanced search offered by Britannica.com when we look at the use of electronic archives for the support of foreign-language text production.

Additional online encyclopedias

If you want to use a different online encyclopedia, try one of the following:

- Encarta Online (http://encarta.msn.com) is a rather large appetiser to Microsoft's multimedia CD-ROM encyclopedia.
- Encyclopedia.com (http://www.encyclopedia.com) contains about 17,000 articles from the Concise Columbia Electronic Encylopedia.
- CIA World Factbook (http://www.odci.gov/cia/publications/factbook/) is more like an almanac or gazetteer than an encyclopedia, but remains a prime source of country-specific information with extensive statistical data and maps on all the countries of the globe. And yes, CIA stands for Central Intelligence Agency.

Merriam-Webster Collegiate Dictionary online

The compete version of the Merriam-Webster Collegiate Dictionary is available online at http://www.m-w.com.

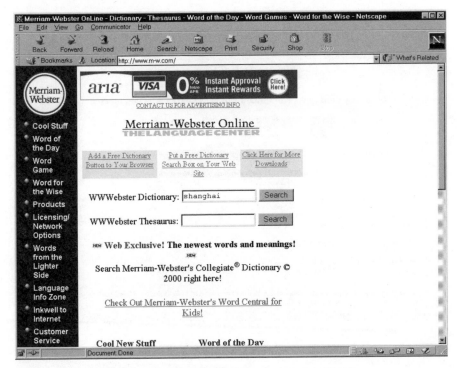

Figure 24. Merriam-Webster Online – Search form

You can search either the dictionary or the thesaurus. Simply enter your search term(s), and click the Search button.

OneLook Dictionaries – A meta-dictionary

OneLook Dictionaries (http://www.onelook.com) is a search platform allowing you to search simultaneously about 600 word lists, glossaries, dictionaries and databases.

Similar to the meta-search engines mentioned in Chapter 4, OneLook directs your query to a multitude of resources, displaying the results arranged by category. The dictionaries queried by OneLook cover a wide range of subject matters, from agricultural biotechnology to Yiddish expressions, from anatomy to mythology. You therefore have to pay close attention to the source of the translation or definition displayed and to the credibility of that source.

PC Webopedia

What the *Encyclopaedia Britannica* is to general reference works, the PC Webopedia (http://www.pcwebopedia.com) is to the world of specialized online encyclopedias. PC Webopedia is a monolingual (English) reference work for

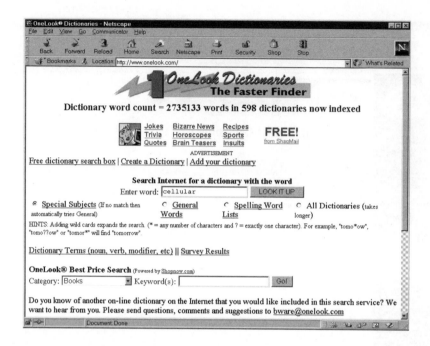

Figure 25. OneLook Dictionaries –Search form

information and communication technology. It contains a multitude of ICT terms, including elaborate and easy-to-understand definitions. The articles are closely interconnected through hyperlinks, and external web resources are referenced as well.

There are two ways of accessing the data stored in Webopedia's database: searching for a keyword, and browsing by categories.

In order to search for any given term, simply enter it in the search box and click on the Go! button. A matching entry will be displayed on the screen. If no article exactly matching your query can be found, a list of articles containing fuzzy matches of your search term will be displayed. If you want to browse Webopedia's contents by category, simply select the category and click the Go! button. The list that appears shows the first and second levels of Webopedia's term categories. The entries in Webopedia usually consist of the term, its definition and links to the related (master or sub-) categories, to the related term and to related websites. In addition, terms that appear in the definition and are also stored as main entries in Webopedia are also hyperlinks, allowing the user to build up a network of terms. Many articles also offer a graphic representation of the term featured.

Webopedia extensions for E-commerce and ISPs

The high-quality, comprehensiveness and timeliness of the contents on PC

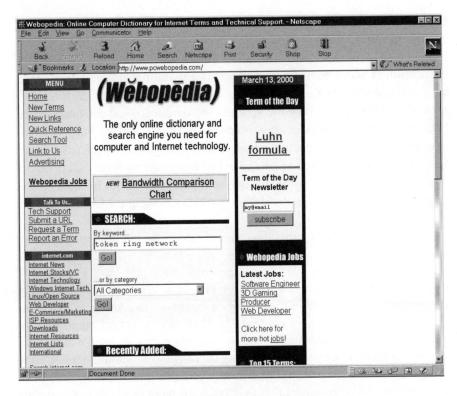

Figure 26. PC Webopedia – Homepage

Webopedia have made it a success story. PC Webopedia has also given rise to two features that deal with more specific ICT aspects. These are:

- the e-commerce glossary at http://e-comm.webopedia.com, which focuses on the terminology of electronic business and electronic commerce;
- the ISP glossary at http://isp.webopedia.com, which covers the main terminology of Internet service providers.

Multilingual terminology databases

In addition to the hundreds of dictionaries and thousands of term collections or glossaries, there are some reliable terminology databases available on the web. More than just a list of terms and definitions as found in glossaries, these databases contain a wide range of terminological information such as synonyms, grammatical categories, context examples, cross-references and source information. In the following, we describe two terminology databases maintained by international organizations: the European Union's multilingual database Eurodicautom, and the International Telecommunications Union's Termite.

Eurodicautom – The EU's multilingual database at your fingertips

Eurodicautom (*dictionnaire automatique*) is a multilingual terminology data-base maintained by the European Commission's Translation Service. Its origins go back to 1976, and it now incorporates the terminological databases of the Council of Europe (TIS, see http://tis.consilium.eu.int/) and the European Parliament (Euterpe, see http://muwi.trados.com/Nav/asp/MainPageConstruction.asp). Both TIS and Euterpe can be searched using the interface described below. Eurodicautom is accessible for free at http://eurodic.ip.lu. In April 1999 it contained 5.5 million entries and 180,000 abbreviations in the EU's 11 official languages.

A query on Eurodicautom allows you to search for the following types of information:

- *Term, abbreviation or phraseology* Precisely speaking, Eurodicautom consists not of one but of three separate databases. In addition to the terminological database, there are separate databases for abbreviations and for phraseology, the latter focusing on how certain terms are used within word combinations or phrases. By selecting the respective options on the website form, you can designate which database you want to search.
- *Enter words/abbreviation* This field holds the word or words that you want to search for. If you enter more than one search term, you can combine them in any of the three following ways:

  - *Partial match* If this option has been selected, a Eurodicautom query will also return results that do not exactly match the word or words you entered. For example, if you entered 'phone cellular' and chose the partial-match option, Eurodicautom would return, amongst others, the entry 'cellular -phone' but also the term 'phone switch'. Partial matches can be helpful if you are seeking a multiword term, especially if you are not exactly sure about the single word occurring in the term.
  - *All words* This option represents a classic Boolean AND search, which means that you are looking for database entries that contain all the words you entered, no matter what order they occur in. If you chose this option for the above query, 'phone switch' would not show up in the result list.
  - *'As is'* This option represents a phrase search, i.e. the words you entered must be matched exactly (same order, all words) by the terms in the database. Only these exact or perfect matches will show up.

- *Source language* Select the source language for your query by clicking on the relevant entry in this list. You can only select one source language at a time. All official EU languages are available.
- *Target language* The target languages comprise all official EU languages

as well. Unlike the source language field, more than one target language can be selected by pressing the Ctrl key and then clicking on the relevant languages.

- *Display additional info* In this box you can select what kind of information you want to see in the query results, as well as the term in the source and target languages. This includes definitions, example of phraseology, references, dates and information on the author of the entry.

- *Subject code(s)* You can use the subject or domain code of a given term as a filter for your query. You can select more than one domain (Ctrl+click). Your query will only search through entries belonging to the selected domain(s).

- *Term base* This option is not available for users external to the European Commission's Translation Service. Internally, it allows individual access to either Eurodicautom or Euterpe, the European Parliament's database.

- *How many?* By selecting one of the options in this list you can determine how many entries are shown on the results screen. The default setting is 10. Displaying more results will lead to longer processing times.

- *Truncation* This option allows you to search for words whose spelling is very close to your keyword. Generally, truncation is applied only if there is no answer to your query. For example, if no entry matching the search term 'development' is found, 'develop' would also be included in the search. You may also activate truncation for all cases by clicking on the Always

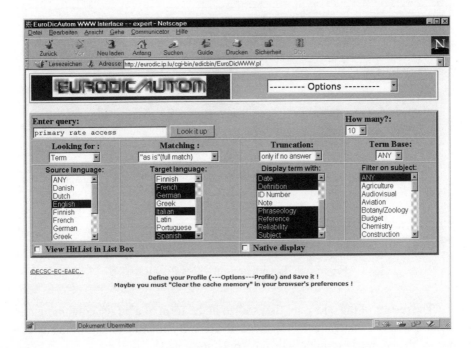

Figure 27. Eurodicautom – Search form

button. Clicking on the button Never will deactivate the truncation option. In the query results, entries that meet the truncation criterion are displayed after the entries that have been found without truncation.

• *Look it up* Clicking on this command button starts the database query.

We may now carry out a sample search. Here Eurodicautom is being used within a multilingual translation project on digital telephony. The term in question is 'primary rate interface'. In addition to equivalents in French, German, Italian and Spanish, a definition is needed to clarify the concept. A phraseology sample would also be helpful to see how the term is used in its syntactic context. The fields 'Reference', 'Author' and 'Date' may also be selected to help identify the quality and reliability of the information provided by Eurodicautom. No subject is selected, since in Eurodicautom it is not always clear what domain a term might belong to.

Since we are looking for a multiword term and not a combination of the three words, the option 'as is (full match)' is selected. No truncation is needed, and the number of results to be displayed at first is limited to 10. The query is activated by clicking on the 'Look it up' button.

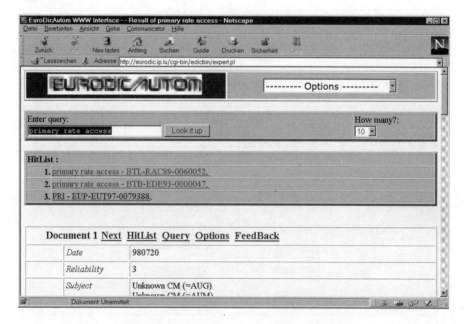

Figure 28. Eurodicautom – Results hit list

The results of the query are first shown in the form of a hit list containing all database entries matching the search parameters. By clicking on one of the listed terms, the complete terminological entry is presented.

Termite - Standardized terminology from the International Telecommunications Union

Termite is the multilingual terminology database of the International Telecommunications Union (ITU). It is a good example of the specialized encyclopedic and linguistic information that can be found on the Internet. The ITU is the agency of the United Nations in charge of co-ordinating global telecommunications activities. It is headquartered in Geneva, Switzerland. Termite is one of a multitude of resources to be found on ITU'S website (http://www.itu.int). It has been maintained since 1979 by the Terminology, References and Computer Aids to Translation Section (Conference Department, General Secretariat). Termite contains about 60,000 entries (as at February 2000) in English, French, Spanish and Russian (transliterated).

Access to Termite is free. Its URL is http://www.itu.int/search/wais/Termite/index.html.

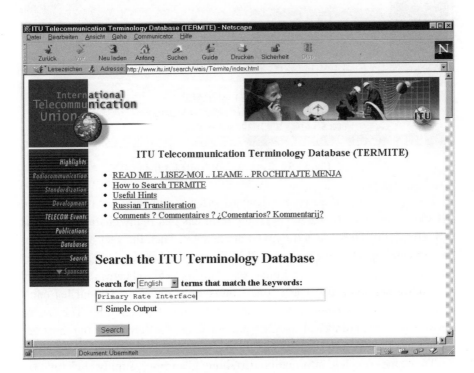

Figure 29. Termite – Search form

To search for terms in Termite, simply select the source language (the results will be presented in all available target languages), type your keyword(s) in the search box, and click on the Search button. You can use an asterisk to perform a generic search. Thus, searching for 'tele*' lists all entries starting with 'tele', such as 'telecommunications', 'television' or 'satellite television'. The search is case-insensitive, and accents and special characters can be omitted.

Try searching for the multiword term 'Primary Rate Interface'.

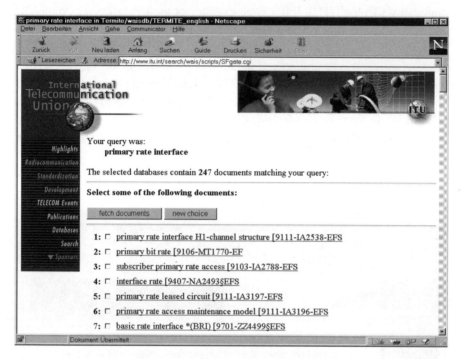

Figure 30. Termite – Results hit list

In response to your query, the database offers a numbered list of terms. The list shows the first 50 characters (if the term has that many characters) of the full term, followed by an acronym (if applicable). Then the year and month of the last entry update are given, as well as a serial number consisting of a combination of two letters and four digits. A section sign (§) indicates that this entry provides a definition (in at least one language) of the term. The hit list entry ends by showing the languages presented in the entry (E, F, S or R). The entries are sorted by the number of matches per entry, i.e. the entry with the most occurrences of the keyword appears at the top of the hit list.

To see the complete information pertaining to an entry, simply click on it (in this example the entry selected was 'primary rate access,' which is synonymous with 'primary rate interface').

As you can see, the entry structure is rather lean, containing the term, a definition, source information and a field named Context or Remarks in which different kinds of information can be given (in this case a reference to the domain, ISDN, to which the term belongs).

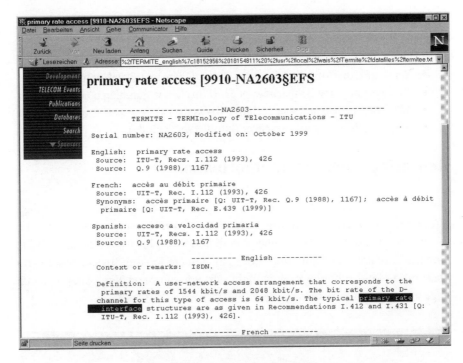

Figure 31. Termite – Term entry

The value of Termite is that it contains terms that have appeared in ITU printed glossaries since 1980 and thus in many cases represent internationally standardized terminology. Further, the terms can be double-checked using the source information given for the terms in the database. This makes it a very reliable source for terminological information.

In addition to Termite, the ITU offers a database called Sancho. Sancho is the oddly pieced-together abbreviation for ITU-T Sector Abbreviations and defiNitions for a teleCommunications tHesaurus Oriented. It is an online database that offers terms and above all, definitions taken from a variety of ITU publications. Its URL is http://www.itu.int/sancho/index.htm.

Newspaper and magazine archives

Electronic newspaper and magazine archives are another very useful resource available on the WWW. A list of newspapers, searchable and browsable by geographic location, can be found at www.ipl.org/reading/news/.

Most of the newspapers and magazines with an online presence offer access to previous online and sometimes also offline editions. Searching the most recent editions is usually free of charge. To dig deeper into the archives, some online archives make you dig deep into your pockets by paying for reading, printing or downloading full articles. The websites that we are going to look at here are all free of charge. They are:

- *Newsweek*, the American magazine (http://www.newsweek.com)
- *The Guardian*, the British newspaper (http://www.guardian.co.uk)
- *ABC*, the Spanish newspaper (http://www.abc.es)
- *Die Welt*, the German newspaper (http://www.welt.de).

Retrieving background information

Online archives can be used during the reception and transfer phases of a translation (e.g. to retrieve missing background information) and during the formulation phase to check whether certain terms or phrases can be used in the language you are translating into. Let's say you are looking for information on the subject of biotechnology. You might start your quest on Newsweek's search page at http://search.newsweek.com.

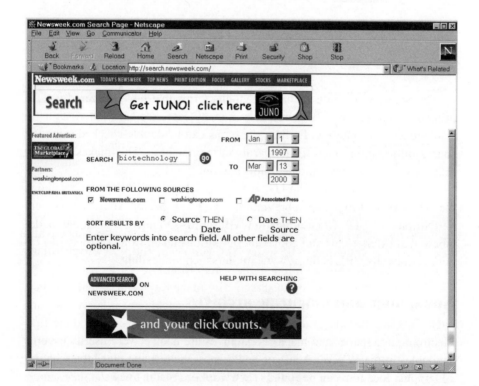

Figure 32. Newsweek – Search form

As you can see, the archive contains articles not only from *Newsweek* but also from the online edition of *The Washington Post*, and two weeks of newsfeed from the news agency Associated Press (AP). Activate the check box to select the sources you want to use for your search. If you entered more than one keyword, they will automatically be connected with the AND operator, i.e. all documents containing all the keywords entered will be returned.

By default, the search results are sorted first by source and then by data (in reverse chronological order). In addition to the source of the documents, the title, authors, date of first publication and first lines are displayed. Click on the highlighted title to see the full text. Using your browser's 'Find in page' feature (Ctrl+F) you can then search the article for keywords, for example to see whether it is acceptable to use 'biotech' instead of 'biotechnology'. In addition to the basic search, Newsweek.com also offers an advanced search, which allows you to select sections (subject areas) for your search.

As you can see, using online archives is an easy and fast way of finding background information. There are also all kinds of scientific journals (e-journals) on the WWW that are valuable sources of specialized information. However, many of them are only available through commercial database suppliers such as Nexis-Lexis or Dialog, which charge a hefty fee. There are also several journals that require registration and may only be accessible to accredited professionals. See http://lexis-nexis.com/lncc/sources/ and http://products.dialog.com/products/ for more information on these commercial information providers.

Confirming terms and phrases

Online archives can also be used for checking terminology and phraseology, especially when you are translating into a foreign language. This means using the archives as corpora.

Let's assume you are writing a text in English and would like to use the expression 'to implement a strategy', but as a non-native English speaker, you are not sure whether this is correct. Your favourite native speaker is not available to answer your question, so try *The Guardian* (http://www.guardian.co.uk). Click on Archive to bring up the search form.

Simply enter the phrase you want to verify in the Keyword(s) field and click on the Search button. If there are any documents matching your query, they are listed showing the title of the article, the date of its publication, and the first paragraph of the article. Since your search phrase does not necessarily have to show up in this first paragraph, you can display the full text by clicking on the title. Using your browser's 'Find in page' feature (Ctrl+F) you can then search the article for the phrase that you want to confirm.

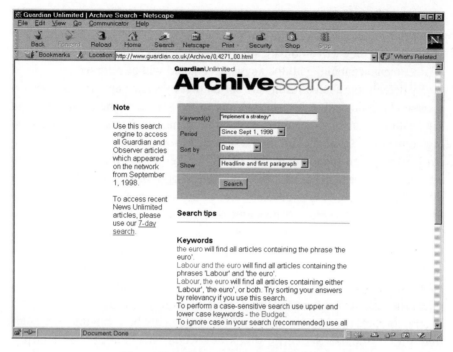

Figure 33. *The Guardian* – Search form

Using proximity operators

As mentioned above, proximity operators can narrow down your online search in a very efficient way. Many online archives offer this search feature. Here we will look at the Spanish daily *ABC* and Germany's *Die Welt*.

ABC's search form is available at http://www.abc.es/busquedas/busquedas.asp.

In addition to the Boolean operators AND, OR and NOT and the phrase search (put phrase in quotes), the online search form of *ABC* also accepts the operator NEAR. The NEAR search is basically an AND search, meaning that the document has to contain all the search terms. In addition, these search terms cannot be further than 50 words apart. The span between the search terms combined with the NEAR operator varies from archive to archive. The German newspaper *Die Welt*, for example, also provides the NEAR operator for its advanced search. You can access the online archive at http://archiv.welt.de. Click on Erweiterte Suche to call up the advanced search form.

The operator connecting the search terms is selected using a drop-down box. You can use AND, OR, NOT and NEAR. A phrase search is also possible (simply put the phrase in quotes). You can also restrict your search to specific sections of the online edition of the newspaper (e.g. politics, science, sports).

The NEAR operator looks for occurrences of the search terms within 10 words of each other, allowing for a more flexible search than the phrase search.

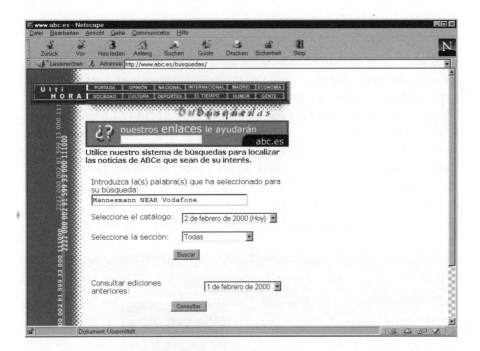

Figure 34. *ABC* – Search form

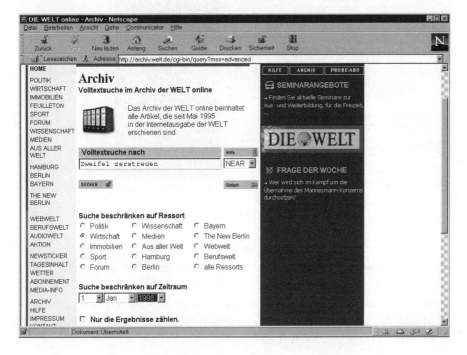

Figure 35. *Die Welt* – Advanced search form

Let's say you need to translate the expression 'to dispel doubts' into German. As is usually the case with collocations, you will have no problem translating one part of the word combination, in this case 'doubt' (*Zweifel*). But what about the other part, the collocator? You will probably come up with a series of solutions, such as '*Zweifel zerstören*', '*Zweifel auflösen*', '*Zweifel vertreiben*' or '*Zweifel zerstreuen*'. Again, a native speaker could help you with this problem, but they are not always available. So use the expertise of German native speakers provided in the online archive of *Die Welt*. Enter 'Zweifel zerstreuen', and select the NEAR operator. Click on the Suchen button to start your query. The query brings up two articles in which the two search terms appear within a distance of no more than 10 words of each other (it is not important what order they appear in). Click on the title of the article to display the full text.

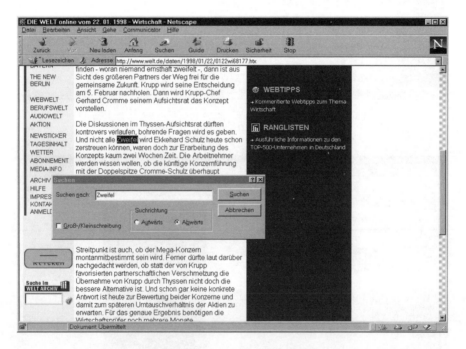

Figure 36. *Die Welt* – Full article

Again, use the 'Find in page' feature of the browser to look for the occurrence of your search terms. In this case, looking for 'Zweifel' brings you to a sentence ('*und nicht alle Zweifel wird Ekkehard Schulz heute schon zerstreuen können...*'), which shows that your proposal for translating this collocation is a valid one. As you can see, a phrase search would not have found this occurrence, since the collocational span comprises several words.

Tasks

✓ What is an OPAC?
✓ Use the OPAC of the Bibliothèque Nationale de France to find French legal dictionaries.
✓ Use PC Webopedia to find out what the difference is between a LAN and a WAN.
✓ Use the archive of *ABC* to find texts concerning mobile phones.
✓ Use Termite to find out what the following abbreviations stand for: GSM, ISDN, WAP.
✓ Use Yahoo to find online newspapers in your first foreign language. Bookmark them in your browser.
✓ What is the capital of Tuvalu? And what is the country's ISO code?

Further reading and Internet links

The European Translation Platform: http://www2.echo.lu/etp/
The Translation Journal: http://www.accurapid.com/journal/
The Translator's Home Companion: http://www.rahul.net/lai/companion.html
Library of Congress (OPAC): http://catalog.loc.gov
Bibliothèque Nationale de France (OPAC): http://catalogue.bnf.fr
Amazon.com: http://www.amazon.com
Barnes & Noble online: http://barnesandnoble.com
Britannica online: http://www.britannica.com
CIA World Factbook: http://www.odci.gov/cia/publications/factbook/
Encyclopedia.com: http://www.encyclopedia.com
MS Encarta: http://encarta.msn.com
Merriam-Webster online: http://www.m-w.com
OneLook Dictionaries: http://www.onelook.com
PC Webopedia: http://www.pcwebopedia.com
E-commerce glossary: http://e-comm.webopedia.com
Internet Service Provider glossary: http://isp.webopedia.com
Eurodicautom: http://eurodic.ip.lu
Termite: http://www.itu.int/search/wais/Termite/index.html
ABC: http://www.abc.es
Die Welt: http://www.welt.de
The Guardian: http://www.guardian.co.uk
Los Angeles Times: http://www.latimes.com
Newsweek: http://www.newsweek.com

6. The world on a disk – Translation resources on CD-ROM

While the Internet is an online medium, a CD-ROM (compact disc, read-only memory) offers information offline. This means you can access the information locally without having to establish a network connection. CD-ROMs (and their latest offspring, DVDs, or digital versatile disks) are very similar to regular audio CDs. In order to access the information, you need a CD-ROM drive, which is an optical storage device. That means that the information it stores is read and written via a laser. Their many advantages over print media have made CD-ROMs a prime platform for the presentation of reference works of all kinds.

The goals of this chapter are:

- to show how CD-ROMs work;
- to discuss the advantages of CD-ROMs as storage media for information resources in general and for translation resources specifically;
- to categorize the kind of translation resources available on CD-ROM;
- to describe the general search strategies for CD-ROM-based information;
- to provide examples of encyclopedias, encyclopaedic dictionaries, and dictionaries on CD-ROM and how they can best be used within the translation process.

The advantages of CD-ROMs

Since they are able to store vast amounts of data (in general around 650 Mb, which is 450 times as much as a floppy disk), CD-ROMs are highly suitable for storing multimedia information or huge amounts of textual data. CD-ROMs have long been a popular medium for the distribution of reference works and large databases. The contents of the 32-volume edition of the *Encyclopaedia Britannica*, for example, can be stored on a single CD-ROM. CD-ROMs are also fairly cheap to produce, especially compared with the costs involved in the production of a book. The cost issue (and the general trend toward the digitization of media) has prompted many publishing houses to shift the production of reference works from print to electronic form.

CD-ROMs also provide an efficient way of applying natural human research strategies. This is especially true for translation-related information research.

So what are the advantages of a CD-ROM reference work over one in book form? Or, more generally, what are the advantages of digitized data presentation over printed information? We might consider the following:

- size (try putting the print version of the *Encyclopaedia Britannica* in your coat pocket)

- price (lower production costs)
- multimedia ability (graphics, audio and video sequences are easily integrated)
- fast and comprehensive search (within seconds all articles are searched, and 100 percent of the content is screened)
- various filtering and sorting options
- transferability of the data presented (e.g. data can be copied into word-processed documents or term databases)
- print-on-demand (the contents of the CD-ROM can be printed out if necessary)
- the use of hyperlinks allows for effective networking of entries (for cross-references, synonyms, etc.)
- fast and easy updating (including updating over the Internet).

Translation resources available on CD-ROM

There is a wide variety of translation resources available on CD-ROM. To understand what kinds of reference works there are and how they can be used by translators, it is helpful to look at a typology of reference works. One of the oldest categorizations of reference works comes from D'Alembert who, in the eighteenth century, defined three basic types:

- *dictionnaires de sciences et d'arts* (= *dictionnaires de chose* = *l'encyclopédie*)
- *dictionnaires de langues* (= *dictionnaires de mots*)
- *dictionnaires historiques* (= *dictionnaires de faits*) (Hupka 1989:998).

D'Alembert's typology is still very much reflected in the way reference works are categorized into (linguistic) dictionaries and encyclopedias, a categorization that is still used today to identify the main kinds of reference works. The functions of D'Alembert's historical dictionaries (*dictionnaires historiques*), which contained information on names and places, are today absorbed by general encyclopedias (or by other, less widespread reference works such as almanacs or gazetteers). The general difference between the other two types – *dictionnaires de chose* (encyclopedia) and *dictionnaires de mots* (dictionary) – is that an encyclopedia explains things, whereas a dictionary explains words. In reality, both types of reference work can contain information found in the other type, i.e. a dictionary can contain encyclopedic information, and an encyclopedia can also contain linguistic information.

In addition to these basic types of reference work, a hybrid solution can often be found, especially in Romance-language countries, where a mix between dictionaries and encyclopedias is generally referred to as an 'encyclopedic dictionary'. Such things obviously give information on words and things.

All three – encyclopedias, dictionaries and encyclopaedic dictionaries – can be of either general content, containing information on all branches of knowledge, or specialized content, presenting linguistic and/or encyclopedic information for a restricted discipline only. It is interesting to note that specialized encyclopedias are often referred to as 'dictionaries'.

In addition to the classic types of reference work, modern professional translators also use bibliographic databases and CD-ROMs containing archives of articles from newspapers, magazines and scientific journals.

Figure 37 shows the typology of translation resources on CD-ROM presented in this book.

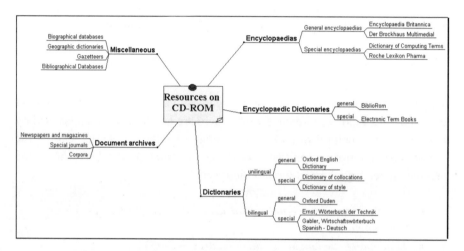

Figure 37. A typology of translation resources on CD-ROM

Encyclopedias

The word 'encyclopedia' comes from the Greek words *egkukloV* (circling, encompassing) and *paideia* (education, learning). It describes a reference work that contains concise summaries of available knowledge. This knowledge can refer to either a wide range of subject matter (provided in general encyclopedias) or to a specific field (provided in specialized encyclopedias). In their more than 2,000 years of history, encyclopedias have never relied on text alone to represent their contents; they have always incorporated other media as well, for example maps or drawings. Over time, diagrams, charts, tables and photographs were added to the printed text. Tables of contents, indexes, and bibliographies further enhance the effectiveness of encyclopedias. Today, with the change from print to electronic representation, encyclopedias commonly feature animated graphics, sound files and video clips. Flexible search features and hyperlinks that network the available knowledge enable the user to search the data stored on the CD-ROM.

Newspapers, magazines and journals

Newspapers, magazines and scientific journals can be a valuable resource for translators trying to get acquainted with a certain subject. They offer information that can be useful during the reception phase of the translation, helping the translator to understand the source text. They can also be used in the formulation phase of a translation, since they present huge collections of parallel texts.

Many newspaper publishers have started to publish annual volumes of their papers on CD-ROM, enabling the reader to search through all the articles of one or more years of newspapers in seconds. For example, if you are preparing for a translation project on water pollution, you can find all the articles that appeared in the *Los Angeles Times* on the subject in 1999 by simply searching for the phrase 'water pollution' in their CD-ROM archive. Within a few seconds you will have gathered a massive amount of data that will allow you to familiarize yourself with the topic in a very short time. If you run the same search in a Spanish newspaper archive on CD-ROM, you will have a series of parallel texts, presenting the terminology and phraseology used by Spanish journalists who have written on the subject.

In addition to newspapers, magazines such as *Time*, *Newsweek* and *Der Spiegel* are available on CD-ROM. Highly specialized journals are actually the sector most active in the production of CD-ROM publications. Almost every topic imaginable has been covered by and for specialists. These technical and scientific journals provide very reliable and informative insights into the subject matters they deal with. Here again, translators can find detailed information on the subjects that they are interested in, including terminology, by searching these electronic archives for keywords. However, these specialized CD-ROM journals are usually very expensive. As in the case of online databases, many CD-ROMs containing the archives of newspapers, magazines and journals are distributed by commercial information providers such as Lexis-Nexis (see http://lexis-nexis.com/lncc/sources/) or Dialog (see http://products.dialog.com/products). You might want to check the website of a particular newspaper if you are interested in finding out whether they offer archives on CD-ROM.

Bibliographical databases

Bibliographical databases on CD-ROM have long been used by librarians and booksellers to find out what books are available on a specific subject. Translators often have to find concise descriptions of a specific subject matter; bibliographical databases on CD-ROM enable them to search for relevant publications. Doing so from your home or office can save considerable time. Once you have found out what print works are of interest, you can use an online catalogue to see whether a library close to you has those books available.

Alternatively, you can order the books via the Internet from one of the many online bookstores.

Strategies for accessing information on CD-ROM

No matter what kind of reference work you use, there are two general approaches to accessing information stored on CD-ROM: browsing and searching. Figure 38 illustrates the two general strategies and their variations.

Accessing electronic information

Browsing	**Searching**
• alphabetical, by entry	• index search, by article title
• thematic, by subject	• full text search, linear
• chronological, by time line	• generic/fuzzy search
• random, by quiz, media type	• Boolean search (AND, OR, NOT)
	• phrase search
	• proximity search (NEAR, ADJ)
	• filtering, by subject, media type, etc.

Figure 38. Types of electronic information access

Browsing the information stored on CD-ROM

Browsing represents a top-down approach to information retrieval. One of the simplest yet most frequently used forms of browsing the contents of an encyclopedia, for example, is simply to read its entries in a linear (alphabetical) order. Most digital reference works provide a button that allows you to 'turn the pages' of the CD-ROM. In addition to going through a CD-ROM alphabetically, you can browse its contents by subject area (e.g. medicine, arts, history, etc.). If you select just one subject area you will only be presented with the entries that have to do with that discipline. This kind of selection allows you to get acquainted quickly with a field in which you are preparing a translation project. A third way of using a reference work is to browse through articles that provide not only text information but information represented using other media types (for example, pictures, video clips, graphs or tables). Many encyclopedias also offer chronological access to information by integrating a time line into their line of features. Most CD-ROMs provide some sort of knowledge quiz that enables you to have some fun while retrieving information from the disk.

Searching for information stored on CD-ROM

While the principle of browsing involves discovering information, strategies for searching are aimed at finding a specific piece of information. In this case, you look for specific keywords or combinations of keywords that, in an ideal situation, identify precisely the entry you are looking for.

Despite a lack of standardization, most reference works offer two types of searching approaches. One is often called a simple or basic search; the other is a more sophisticated advanced search feature.

The simple approach is usually one that looks up a search word that the user enters in an index list. This list contains all the keywords, i.e. the main entries, of an encyclopedia or a dictionary. It may also contain additional keywords entered by the authors of the reference works in order to identify the contents of an article more exactly. Since the software only has to search through the list of indexed keywords, this kind of search is very fast. It will also lead the user to the articles that are most likely to be relevant to the search. For example, if you search for 'Saxophon' in the index list of the Brockhaus encyclopedia you only get one hit, i.e. the article named 'Saxophon'. Of course, the term 'Saxophon' appears in more articles than this one; in fact, it is in a total of 16 articles. But with the simple search function you are not able to find them all.

That is why almost all digital reference works provide a full-text search function. A full-text search not only goes through the list of indexed entries but will also search the full text of all articles stored on the CD-ROM. This is more time-consuming, but it enables the user to conduct a comprehensive search, completely covering all the information that is there.

In addition to providing a full-text search, advanced search features also enable the user to combine several keywords within one search, and also give them the ability to apply search filters. As far as combining keywords is concerned, the possible combinations are represented by Boolean operators and sometimes also by proximity operators.

Boolean operators
The Boolean operators AND, OR and NOT are powerful tools when searching through large amounts of text. For example, if you enter the keywords 'Saxophon' and 'Jazz' in the German Brockhaus CD-ROM edition and connect them with the AND operator, you will find three articles, one of them dealing with the musical style called 'highlife'. However, if you combine 'Saxophon' and 'Jazz' and connect them with the operator NOT you will find only 13 entries

(remember that 16 entries were found for 'Saxophon'). What happened? Well, NOT is an *exclusion* operator. That means if you search for 'Saxophon' but not for 'Jazz' you will only get those articles referring to 'Saxophon' that *do not* include the word 'Jazz'. As we have seen with the AND search, three Brockhaus articles deal with both 'Saxophon' and 'Jazz'; those three are thus excluded in the NOT search. The third Boolean operator, OR, allows you to search for any of the keywords you entered. Picking up the above example again, a search for 'Saxophon' OR 'Jazz' would bring up all encyclopedia articles in which *either* the word 'Saxophon' *or* the word 'Jazz' occurs. On the Brockhaus CD-ROM, this would be a total of 153 entries.

Proximity operators

Sometimes a Boolean search is not precise enough. For example, in the above AND search ('Saxophon' OR 'Jazz') one of the three articles found was the article 'Morrison'. This is a purely coincidental hit, since under 'Morrison' you can find three sections, among them one for American writer Toni Morrison (referring to one of her most famous works, *Jazz*), and another on the Irish rock musician Van Morrison, who among other things plays the saxophone.

In order to determine the relationship and proximity of two or more key-words more precisely, some retrieval software programs offer 'proximity operators' such as NEAR or NEAR BY (i.e. within a few words of each other, no matter what order), ADJ(ACENT) (next to each other, no matter what order) or FOLLOWED BY (next to each other in the order in which the words are entered).

A variation on proximity searches is the 'phrase search'. If you enter several keywords and activate the phrase search function, the program will search for the words you entered in exactly the order you entered them. If, for example you enter *panta reih*, you will find only two matching entries (one on Heraclitus and one explaining his axiom) on the Brockhaus CD-ROM. Phrase searches are also very useful for verifying certain translations, especially when translating into a foreign language. Thus, if you need to translate 'to exchange data' into German and you are not sure whether it should be 'Daten austauschen' or 'Daten wechseln' you simply run a phrase search and you will find text examples for the first solution only. Considering the multitude of texts available on the Brockhaus CD-ROM and the reliability of the work, you can be quite sure that this is the right phrase in German. Clearly, a CD-ROM-based encyclopedia can also be used as a powerful corpus.

Filtering information

In order to state a query even more precisely, search programs also feature various types of filter. A filter reduces the number of entries to be searched by dismissing those that do not meet one or more specified criteria. The Brockhaus

CD-ROM, for example, allows you to use subject areas as filters. To use this, you can search for any given word (e.g. 'Jazz') and have it searched for only in the articles that belong to one or more specific categories (e.g. 'Literatur'). Other filters consist of media types (i.e. images, audio or video clips) or dates (i.e. to search only for articles referring to a specified time frame).

Additional search features
In addition to the above browsing and searching features, there are many other ways of making access to information on CD-ROM much more effective. Here we will run through some of the most useful ones:

- Doing a search from within a different application, e.g. starting a search in a dictionary or encyclopedia by double-clicking on a word in your word-processor. The word you double-click on automatically becomes the keyword to be searched. This feature will usually be automatically added to your word-processor upon installation of the CD-ROM's retrieval program.
- Searching a word within an article by simply double-clicking on it. When you do this, any word in an encyclopedia entry can become a keyword to be searched itself. The word you double-click on does not have to be a hyperlink.
- Copying articles or media files from a reference work onto the clipboard. In many cases you might want to copy an article, or parts of an article, or a table, graph or image associated with an article and reuse it in a word-processor or database (for example, as a definition or context example for a term in your terminology database). Under Windows this kind of transfer is normally done by using the clipboard function. To do this, you select the text you want to copy, press Ctrl+C to copy it onto the clipboard, and then Ctrl+V to paste it into the application. In addition, menu items for copying complete articles and media are available as standard features in most CD-ROM-based reference works.
- Link an entry with other entries through hyperlink. Many articles in encyclopedias, dictionaries, journals, etc. are related to one another. Hyper-links – electronic cross-references – allow lexicographers to make these interconnections between entries visible and the related references immediately accessible (by simply clicking on the hyperlink). Following links to related information on the CD-ROM thus becomes a way of searching as well.
- Adding your own notes to an entry, thus customising the reference work step-by-step.
- Bookmarking entries for faster access to important information.
- Keeping a list of visited entries (history list) to show your search progress and to let you return quickly to information you might need again.
- Finding additional information on the subject of an entry through the use of bibliographical data or links to primary or secondary texts (either on CD-ROM or on the WWW).

Reference works: Two case studies

It is clearly impossible to describe or even list all the dictionaries or encyclopedias that are available on CD-ROM. The easiest way to get an overview of
reference works in a field is to conduct an Internet search, starting with a search
in a virtual bookstore. In the following, two CD-ROMs, the *Oxford English
Dictionary* and the French *Bibliorom*, are presented to give an idea of the general
set-up of multimedia reference works.

The Oxford English Dictionary

The CD-ROM version of the *Oxford English Dictionary* (*OED*) holds the contents of the 20-volume print edition of one of the world's most prestigious
dictionaries. It provides definitions of more than half a million words, and through
almost two and a half million quotations it offers a wealth of information on the
diachronic and synchronic usage of the terms it features.

The CD-ROM version offers a variety of search options, the most basic being the word search. Simply enter the word(s) you are looking for in the search
box and press the Enter key. All entries matching the search term(s) will be
listed. If you click on the list entry you are interested in, the complete article
will be displayed (Figure 39).

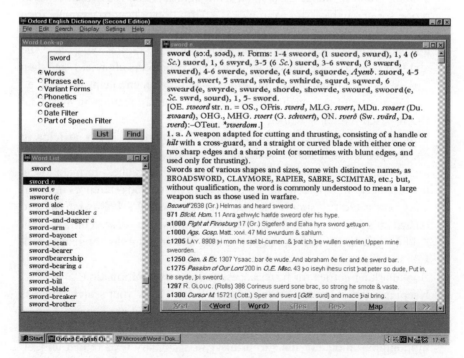

Figure 39. *OED* – Word search form and results

You can also look for phrases by selecting the respective option in the Word Look-up section, which only allows you to search the indexed (i.e. main) entries of the *OED*. To perform a full-text search, select Text Search from the Search menu.

The *OED* lets you use proximity operators to look for search terms that are close to one another. The distance between the words searched for is indicated by a # symbol followed by the number of words to which the distance is to be restricted. The maximum value is 32 words. Proximity searching can be very useful when looking for word combinations without having to bother about articles or adjectives that would render a phrase search useless.

Bibliorom

The French *Bibliorom Larousse* is a small virtual reference library offering several reference works integrated on a single CD-ROM (thus saving you from becoming a 'disk jockey'). The individual resources available are *Le Petit Robert Larousse*, an encyclopedic dictionary containing more than 80,000 articles, the *Thésaurus Larousse*, a dictionary of quotations and three bilingual dictionaries (French-English, English-French, Spanish-English, English-Spanish, French-German, German-French).

All the resources on the CD-ROM can be searched using the same search form. Any search term or terms entered in the Index or Recherche fields will automatically be looked for in all available reference works. The articles from the different resources are marked by colours.

The entries in *Bibliorom* are completely hyperlinked: simply double-clicking on an article title in the index section will bring up the complete article in the right window. The interface is organized in the frame style used in many worldwide web sites. There are also many hyperlinks in the complete articles. They are highlighted in red and can be activated by clicking on them. You can also make any word appearing in the article your new search term by right-clicking on it and selecting the resource in which to look for the term.

In addition to the Index search that covers only the titles of the main articles, *Bibliorom* offers a full-text search. Click on the Recherche tab to bring the full-text search form onto the screen. You can simply enter your search term or search phrase in the search field and click on Rechercher to start your search. This will activate a full-text search for the expressions entered.

Clicking on the Recherche Approfondie button in the lower left-hand corner of the interface will bring up a search form for a more detailed search. This lets you define in which reference work the search is to be conducted and whether you want to include certain multimedia elements in your search (e.g. audio or video sequences). By selecting the Médias tab you can also restrict your search to articles containing multimedia elements. Results from a search in *Bibliorom* can be printed out or copied into the clipboard to be re-used in, for example, a Word document.

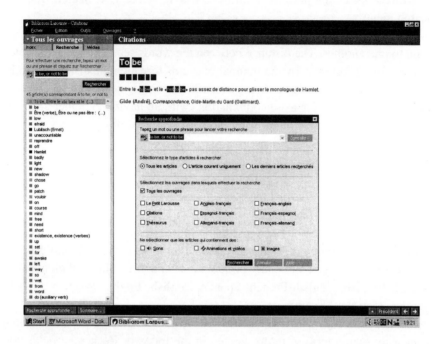

Figure 40. *Bibliorom* – Full text search form

Strategies for integrating electronic reference works

Integrating several reference works on a single CD-ROM is one approach to improving the use of optical discs. It saves you the trouble of having to change the discs in your CD-ROM drives every time you need to look up some information in a different work. A German reference work working in the same way as *Bibliorom* is the LexiROM offered by Microsoft, which includes several reference works on one CD-ROM (see LexiROM: http://www.microsoft.com/ GERMANY/homeoffice/lexirom/default.htm).

A similar approach is taken by the PC-Bibliothek (see http://www.duden. bifab.de /produkte/pcbib/), which integrates several reference works from Brockhaus, Duden, Meyer and Langenscheidt on the same platform. Individual resources like the *Duden Oxford Großwörterbuch Englisch*, *Duden Universalwörterbuch*, or the Duden stylistic dictionary are distributed on individual CD-ROMs but can be copied onto the hard disk of the computer and accessed using one and the same search interface.

If it is not possible for you to get all the reference works you need on a single CD-ROM or within the same product series, you can use a type of software called Virtual CD to save you the trouble of changing the CD-ROMs. Virtual CD (see http://www.virtualcd-online.com/ and http://www.cdrom-emulator.com/index1.htm) lets you copy the complete CD-ROM onto your hard disk (while at the same time compressing it to save storage capacity). Each CD-ROM copied onto the hard disk is assigned a virtual drive letter, so that when trying to access the CD-ROM your computer will look for the CD-ROM not in the real drive but in the virtual one. All you have to do is let the computer know in which virtual drive the respective CD-ROM can be found.

Tasks

✓ What are the general advantages of reference works on CD-ROM?
✓ Describe the various strategies for accessing information stored on CD-ROM.
✓ Put together a list of criteria for the evaluation of reference works on CD-ROM.
✓ Use Amazon.com to retrieve a list of encyclopedias and dictionaries on CD-ROM.
✓ Download a demo version of virtual CD-ROM drive software and create a virtual CD-ROM on your computer's hard disk.
✓ Build a typology of reference works for your working languages and areas of specialization (see Figure 37).

Further reading and Internet links

Hausmann, F.J., O. Reichmann, H.E. Wiegand, L. Zgusta (eds) (1989) *Wörterbücher – Dictionaries – Dictionnaires. Ein internationales Handbuch zur Lexikographie* (Handbücher zur Sprach- und Kommunikationswissenschaft, vol. 5.1), Berlin & New York: De Gruyter.
Holderbaum, A. (1999) 'Kriterien der Evaluation elektronischer Wörterbücher – am Beispiel der CD-ROM-Version des Oxford Advanced Learner's Dictionary of Current English', *AREAS – Annual Report on English and American Studies* 17. Trier: WVT Wissenschaftlicher Verlag Trier. 365-386.
Winchester, S. (1998) *The Professor and the Madman: A tale of murder, insanity, and the making of the Oxford English Dictionary*, New York: HarperCollins.

Encyclopaedia Britannica Online: (articles on 'dictionary' and 'encyclopedia'): http://www.britannica.com
Lexis-Nexis: http://lexis-nexis.com/lncc/sources/
Dialog: http://products.dialog.com/products
Oxford English Dictionary: http://www.oed.com
LexiROM: http://www.microsoft.com/germany/produkte/overview.asp?siteid=10389
PC-Bibliothek: http://131.99.21.138/presse/artikel/digital.html
Virtual CD-ROM drives: http://www.cdrom-emulator.com/index1.htm and http://www.virtualcd-online.com/

7. Computer-assisted terminology management

Professional translation is mostly technical translation. A technical translator is forced to keep up with the many fast and significant changes that are taking place in the fields of information technology, manufacturing, business, medicine, biotechnology and so on. However, it would be unrealistic to expect a translator to be a natural expert in all these fields. In fact, considering the incredible amount of information available today, such expertise would be simply impossible.

Similarly unrealistic is the idea that when preparing a translation project a translator can easily become an expert in any given matter by spending months researching the subject. Of course, they need to have a basic understanding of the field. If, for example, you are going to translate the manual of a sophisticated e-commerce program you had better be familiar with computers, software, the Internet and some business terms. But you probably will not have to be an expert in database design or transaction security. You will simply have to be an expert in quickly finding the information that you are lacking, be it encyclopedic or linguistic.

That said, it is almost never possible to find *the* right dictionary for a topic, or to find *the* standard textbook, or even to find a considerable number of parallel texts that can be trusted. In this regard the search for correct terminology – that is, for the technical vocabulary of a discipline – can be especially time-consuming. According to some studies, the search for terminology (or 'terminology mining') can take up to 75 percent of a translator's time (Arntz & Picht 1989:234).

In order to use your time efficiently you should set up a database very early in your career. This should be a database in which you gather all the terminology that you come across during your studies and in your professional life. Such 'terminology management' (TM) basically enables you to put together your own specialized encyclopedic dictionary on your PC. It can best be done by using computer-based management systems.

Terminology management is a generic term for the documentation, storage, manipulation and presentation of specialized vocabulary. The terminology covered is usually that of a given discipline or sub-discipline or the terms needed for a specific translation project. Owing to the amount of terminology to be managed and the need to provide fast and easy access to the data stored, terminology management is assisted by information and communication technology. In order to gather terminological data, terminologists or translators use electronic resources such as the Internet, CD-ROM or electronic corpora. For the extraction of terminology, text analysis software (see Chapter 8) or extraction programs (see Chapter 9) are used. The management of the terminology itself is also done using a computer and specific software. By analogy with the distinction between lexicology and lexicography, the design, compilation, use and evaluation of collections of terminology is called 'terminography'.

In this chapter we will briefly discuss the various ways of managing terminology. We will then see in detail how to use a specific TM system, Trados' MultiTerm '95 Plus. This chapter can only give the reader a rather compressed insight into the complex area of computer-assisted TM. For an in-depth description of the subject see Austermühl and Coners (forthcoming).

Forms of terminology management – from file cards to hypermedia systems

There are several ways of keeping track of a specific discipline's specialized words and expressions, i.e. its terminology. Here we will list the various options available to translators (or terminologists), indicating their advantages and disadvantages. We start with the least sophisticated approaches, gradually moving up to the technically more advanced forms.

In general, the following methods can be used to keep track of terminology:

- file cards
- lists in word-processors (e.g. WinWord or Word Perfect)
- spreadsheets (e.g. Excel or Lotus 1.2.3)
- database management systems (e.g. Access or Approach)
- terminology management systems (e.g. MultiTerm or Termstar)
- hypermedia systems (e.g. PC Webopedia).

We will look at each of these in turn.

TM using file cards

For many translation students, the use of file cards is their first contact with TM methods. The advantages of file cards are limited. Indeed, the list of their shortcomings shows why they should no longer be used, neither in translator training nor in the 'real world'.

Advantages
- easy to handle
- (simple) graphics can be added.

Disadvantages
- limited options for searching and sorting (usually you search for and sort by the main term in one language; it is not possible to search for certain words in a definition or in a context example)

- slow access
- time-consuming data maintenance
- limited space.

TM using a word-processor

The first electronic form of TM is usually one involving word-processing soft-ware. In most cases you try to sort your terminological data in tables, with the column headers representing the different fields or types of information (such as Term, Definition, Context, Synonym, etc.). You sort the table and then use the word processor Find option (in WinWord easily activated by the Ctrl+F key combination) to search for a given term. For short tables, you can also simply browse through the entries.

The use of word-processors to store terminology has several advantages that make it quite popular among translation professionals. Your client might also provide you with an existing glossary of this kind.

Advantages
- no need to buy and learn a new application
- widely used; no problems with compatibility
- easy co-operation between text production and terminology management; all you need to do is open the text and the terminology files at the same time, then you just switch between the two. If your screen is big enough you might actually be able to put both files on the screen simultaneously.

Disadvantages
- limited options for presenting and sorting the data on screen (especially if you want to use numerous fields, i.e. columns)
- since the search is linear, it is slow in large files.

TM using a spreadsheet application

The use of spreadsheet applications such as MS Excel has become very popular in translation agencies. This probably because Excel spreadsheets are used by many software companies to record the translation of their programs, e.g. their graphical user interfaces (GUI).

Advantages
- no need to buy and learn a new application
- widely used; no problems with compatibility
- easy co-operation between text production and terminology management; just start both applications, then switch between them using the task bar or the Alt+Tab key combination.

Disadvantages

- limited options for presenting and sorting data on screen (especially if you want to use numerous fields, i.e. columns)
- since the search is linear, it is slow in large files
- poor representation of the search result (only the cell which contains the searched word is highlighted, not the word itself).

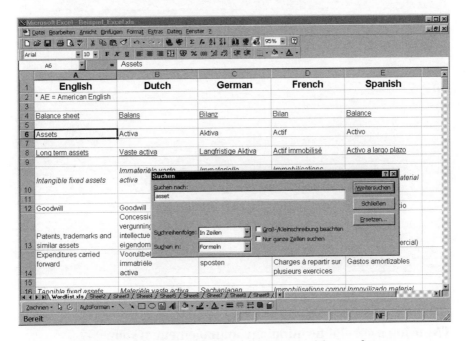

Figure 41. Managing terminology with spreadsheet software

TM using a database management system

Database management systems (DBMS) such as MS Access are highly sophisticated programs that can be used for a variety of tasks such as storing and maintaining client addresses, managing orders and projects, and so on. Basically, translators using a DBMS benefit from the universality of these applications and their manifold functions. They might, however, be put off by the bewildering possibilities these programs offer.

Advantages

- provides a variety of features
- covers different areas (e.g. managing addresses)
- flexible search and sort options
- fast search
- easy data input.

Disadvantages

- the variety of features that can be confusing
- translation-specific features are not automatically available (e.g. automatic look-up of terms, importing data into the word-processor).

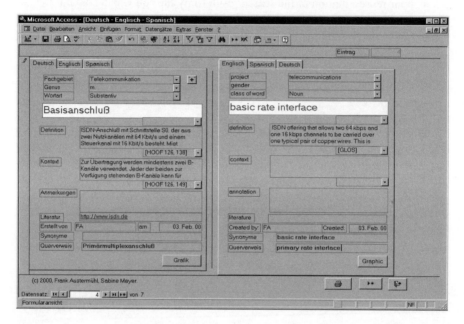

Figure 42. Managing terminology with a database management system

TM using a special terminology management system

The above advantages and disadvantages clearly indicate that the use of database systems is the most effective solution. Yet the sometimes overwhelming range of program features means that universal database management systems are not yet widely used by translators. Instead, market dominance has been gained by customized solutions, i.e. database management systems that have been designed for translators as the prime target groups. There is a great variety of these terminology management systems, among them products called CATS, Termstar and MultiTerm. The last-mentioned will be described in detail below.

Advantages

- suited to translation-specific routines (for example, looking up terms from within a word-processor, importing data from the database into the word-processor)
- concentrates on translation-relevant functions
- fast and flexible search
- automated communication between database and word-processor.

Disadvantages
- limited usage (no address or order management)
- high price.

TM using a hypermedia system

Hypermedia systems are based on the same technology used for web documents (HTML). They have become a very popular form for the presentation of terminological data, especially since they permit the easy linking of database contents and the addition of multimedia information and large text documents. These programs can be used online or offline. However, hypermedia systems are very time-consuming in the input of terminological data (for which you would have to use a web editor). That is why they are mainly used for data representation only. The input is done using the above-mentioned database or terminology management systems. The HTML documents can then be created automatically through a specific export command or an additional software utility.

Advantages
- easy to learn and use
- universal usage and availability (if used online)
- compatibility with word-processor
- extensive options for linking elements (e.g. encyclopedic information and language data).

Disadvantages
- limited search and sort options
- time-consuming creation.

Managing terminological data using terminology management systems

Before you decide to buy and use a terminology management system (TMS) you should find out whether it meets your specific needs. To evaluate the suitability of a TMS, a simple check of the application's options and features is not enough. Your evaluation process should also reflect your standard working routines. In this context, special importance must usually be attached to importing language data and converting existing terminology to the respective database format, as well as the interaction or communication between a database and a word-processor.

Criteria for evaluating terminology management systems

Working on a translation largely means searching for terminology. Translation-related terminology research (and management) is carried out in a number of ways depending on the kind of project or task to be performed. Basically, we can distinguish between three working scenarios:

- creating and maintaining terminology using internal or external data;
- searching terminology before and during the translation process;
- exporting terminological data as dictionaries, glossaries or word lists (electronic and print).

Using these working routines as a basis, we can formulate what is required of an efficient TMS:

- easy creation of new databases (using an 'electronic assistant', for example);
- extensive and easy-to-define retrieval options;
- easy-to-use import options for external databases;
- communication with a word-processing application;
- (predefined) export options.

The general user-friendliness of the software might be added as an overriding criterion. This would cover such things as an easy-to-learn interface, the use of macros to access important commands easily, compatibility with other software applications, a comprehensive online help system and well-written documentation.

Managing terminological data with MultiTerm

Here we will discuss the use of terminology management systems in greater detail. The application of Trados' MultiTerm '95 Plus will be described as a case study. A demo version of the program can be downloaded at http://www.trados.com. You should download this version and work with it while you read through this chapter (using the sample file Guidemo.mtw).

MultiTerm runs under the Windows user interface, making the program easy to use for those already familiar with Windows applications. Once you have started the program and opened a database, the main MultiTerm window will appear on your screen. As with other Windows-based applications, the screen is divided into four main areas:

- *Title bar and menu bar* The title bar shows the name of the database that is currently open. It also tells you which mode you are currently in (View or Edit). The menu bar displays MultiTerm's menus, which can be activated by clicking on the menu with the mouse or holding the ALT key and pressing the letter that is underlined in the menu name. The menu opens and shows a list of options that can also be selected by using either the mouse or the keyboard.

- *Dialogue bar* The dialogue bar, also called the index dialogue, is the basic area for your 'dialogue' with MultiTerm. There are two kinds of dialogue bars, depending on whether you are viewing or editing an entry. While MultiTerm is in display mode the index dialogue lets you set the source and target language and provides a box for entering search terms. The current sort term is displayed in red below this box; the previous term appears to the left, the next term to the right. You can browse backwards or forwards through the database either by using the F4 key (previous entry) or the F5 key (next entry) or by clicking directly on the entry names in the index dialogue.
- *Entry window* The entry window shows the actual terminological entry. The first item in the window is always a term in the current source language and any additional information relating to this term, e.g. definition, context. The next item displayed is a term in the current target language with any related information.
- *Message bar* The message bar or message line displays notes about the contents of your database or about the functions you have just performed. The line is displayed in a different colour depending on the kind of message. Information on where you are currently moving the mouse pointer or QuickInfos on menu options are shown in grey. The results of tasks you have just performed are shown in blue, and any program-specific messages relevant to the user are displayed in red. You can remove a message by clicking the message line with the left mouse button. Like most other Windows applications, MultiTerm shows a scroll bar at the right of the window; you can use this to scroll through the current entry.

Building a terminological database

When using a TMS to manage your language data, your first step will be to create a database that will serve as a collection point for all the data you come across in your daily work. TM systems usually come without ready-to-use databases (except for some demonstration databases that will be mentioned below). Thus, one of the main criteria for evaluating a TMS is the system's capabilities for creating databases. Basically, there are two ways to build terminological databases:

- researching terminological data yourself and entering the data into your TMS;
- making use of existing, i.e. external, databases by importing them into your TMS.

The following chapters describe how existing data can be imported into your system. Our main aim here, however, is to create a bilingual database (e.g. for

English and Spanish) that you can use to support your technical translations (here in the field of software localization). Before you start working with MultiTerm you should know what kind of entry structure your database is going to have. That means you have to determine what kind of information you would like to gather in your database. Generally, you will have three types of information to collect:

- *administrative data* e.g. who entered the information, when was it entered, has the information been updated, if so when; what project and/or client the entry refers to;
- *encyclopedic data* e.g. definition of the term, images, logical relationship with other terms, subject area the term belongs to;
- *linguistic data* e.g. grammatical information (gender, part of speech etc.), context example (how is a given term used in a phrase), collocations etc.

The information listed in the above categories should be collected and entered into the database for each of the languages featured. In addition to these language-specific data, information regarding the translation of these terms should be entered. This could include warnings regarding 'false friends', e.g. *do not translate 'ellipsis' with (Spanish) 'elipse' or 'elipsis' but with 'puntos suspensivos'*, or cultural differences with regard to the nature of a given term, e.g. *Note: In the United States, ISDN is less widely distributed than in Europe and used mainly for high-speed Internet access.*

The structure of your terminological entry depends on your individual working situation. If, for example, you are creating a database to be used within the translation department of a medium-sized company, you will have to put in more administrative information than if you are the only person using the database. You should thus first put together a list of the types of information you would like to gather. For example, if you are working as a freelance translator, doing English-Spanish translations (or vice versa) for a number of clients dealing with information technology and automotives, you might want to include the fields shown in Figure 43 in your database.

After you have specified the structure of your database entries, i.e. after having selected the fields for your terminological information, you can create a new database. The database creation process can be divided into three tasks:

1. Creation of a new, empty database, i.e. of a new file
2. Definition of the entry structure, i.e. the selection of the data fields and their characteristics.
3. Entering the terminological data.

Subject (e.g. Telecommunications)	Client (e.g. AT&T)
Project (e.g. ADSL ad)	
Date entered (e.g. 26/02/2000)	Date changed (e.g. 17/06/2000)
English	Spanish
Term (e.g. network management)	Term (e.g. gestión de red)
Term, source (e.g. AT&T ADSL Manual 2/00)	Term, source (e.g. Diccionario de Términos Técnicos)
Part of speech (e.g. noun)	Part of speech (e.g. noun)
Gender	Gender (e.g. female)
Definition (e.g. 'Refers to the broad subject of managing computer networks. There exists a wide variety of software and hardware products that help network system administrators manage a network. Network management covers a wide area, including security, performance, reliability.')	Definition (e.g. 'Funciones relacionadas con la gestión de los recursos de la capa de enlace de datos y la capa física y sus estaciones a través de la red de datos soportada por el sistema híbrido de fibra óptica/coaxial.')
Definition, source (e.g. PC Webopedia)	Definition, source (e.g. ITU, Termite)
Context example or collocation (e.g. CMIS defines a system of network management information services.)	Context example or collocation (e.g. Como CMIP es un protocolo de gestión de red implementado sobre OSI conviene introducir el marco de trabajo OSI en lo que respecta a gestión, ya que será la base para CMIP.)
Context example source (e.g. PC Webopedia)	Context example source (e.g. http://www.arrakis.es/~gepetto/redes/rog08p7.html)
Synonym (e.g. network configuration)	
Cross reference (e.g. network)	Cross reference (e.g. red)
Transfer comment	
Note	

Figure 43. Suggested fields for an English-Spanish TM database

Creating and defining a new database

Before you can start managing your own terminological data using MultiTerm you have to create a new database: Click File/Create New Database. The Database Definition dialogue box opens. This box lets you define the structure and all the relevant settings for your database. If you already have a database open (e.g. a sample database), the settings of this database will automatically be adopted for the new database.

MultiTerm lets you choose between three categories or types of fields – index fields, text fields and attribute fields. Each of these reflects the specific characteristics of the information entered:

- *Index fields* allow fast access to entries. They are by default used for storing

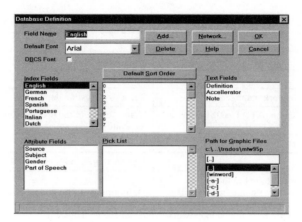

Figure 44. Defining a MultiTerm database

the headwords (terms) of the various languages. MultiTerm allows up to 20 different index fields per database. For each index field you can define a field name, a default font and a default sort order. In the database that we are about to create, only the fields for the terms, English and Spanish, will become index fields.

- *Text fields* carry additional information on individual entries or their head-words. Typical text fields in our terminological database are the definition, context, synonyms, source, transfer comment and note fields. Each data-base can have up to 62 text fields. For each of the text fields you can define a field name and a default font.

- *Attribute fields* also contain additional information, either on a specific data field (index field or text field) or on the whole data entry. Shorter than text fields, they contain classifying information such as the subject area a term belongs to (e.g. information processing, medicine, etc.) and etymological or grammatical information. An important characteristic of attribute fields is that they can only contain values selected from what is known as a 'pick list'. The pick list is a list of values that can later be assigned to the current attribute field. For the attribute field Part of Speech, for example, you would enter the values Verb, Noun, Adjective, etc. Each database can have up to 30 attribute fields. For each of the attribute fields the user must define a field name, a default font and a pick list. In our database the fields Subject, Project, Part of Speech and Gender are suitable attribute fields because their possible content is limited to a range of values that you usually know before you start working with the database. The database definition can always be changed later by using the File/Change Database Definition command.

We can now start building our database.

1. In the Database Definition dialogue box delete all fields except for English

and Spanish. Simply click on the respective fields and then on the Delete button. The fields English and Spanish will be the index fields for your database. They will also host the synonyms of any terms, so you will not need a separate Synonym field. Each index field needs to have a sort order so that the software knows how to store and present the entries of the index field. By selecting an index field and then clicking on the Default Sort Order button you assign the default sorting order to the selected field. However, by simply changing the order of the list, you can create your own sort order.

2. Now create the text fields for your database. The fields Definition and Note can be kept. Delete the field Accelerator. Then add new fields by clicking on the Add button. Enter the name of the field in the Field Name box. Add the fields Context, Transfer Comment, Cross Reference, Source, Date Entered and Date Changed.

3. Finally, you will need four attribute fields: Subject, Client, Project, Part of Speech and Grammar. Delete the fields listed in the dialogue box (except for the field Source) and add the three other fields.

4. Now you have to determine the attributes of these fields, i.e. you must enter the range of values that each field can have in the pick list. The following rules apply to editing the pick list:

    - to delete an entry in the pick list simply click on it and use the Delete or Backspace keys to delete it;
    - each attribute value goes on a line by itself;
    - to insert a new line, press the key combination Ctrl+Enter;
    - the order of the attribute values does not matter; when editing entries, the pick lists are always shown in sorted order;
    - the pick list is displayed in the default font of the current attribute field.

The attribute field should contain the discipline that you specialize in (e.g. telecommunications). Depending on the degree of specialization, you may need to split the subject area in various sub-fields (e.g. not Telecommunications but Mobile Telephony, ISDN, Internet Telephony, etc.).

If you intend to add graphics to your database, MultiTerm needs to know where to look for the files. Click on Path for Graphic Files to indicate the folder in which you have stored (or will store) the graphic files to be used in the database.

Once you have finished the definition of the database, click OK. The Save As dialogue box appears, prompting you to enter a filename and a location for saving the new database.

Creating a new database entry

Now that you have created your database, you can start to enter your terminological data; that is, you can create new database entries. To add a new entry you choose Add Entry from the Edit menu or press the F3 key. In edit mode (which at first is a large blank grey field), pressing the right mouse button calls up a context menu that shows the following options: insert index field, insert text field and insert attribute field. These different types of field can also be selected using the keyboard. Press I to show all the index fields available, T for all the text fields and A for the attribute fields. The list of fields you can now choose from corresponds to the fields you have defined in the Database Definition dialogue. You create an entry by choosing the fields you need one after the other in the order they are supposed to appear in, entering your data and setting parameters on their frequency and accessibility, if desired. You can also go back and insert fields in between the fields you have already created. To do this, place the cursor at the end of the line that immediately precedes the new field you want to create. Finally, click Save to save the current entry in your database and return to View mode.

Creating new entries this way takes quite a lot of time. In order to avoid creating each entry from scratch, MultiTerm also allows you to use 'input models'. These are special entries that can be used as a basis for creating new entries. In other words, they serve as a 'model' of the common structure that all entries should have. This applies to the order of fields, how often a field may appear, whether a field is mandatory, optional, multiple, etc.

You can define and edit a model in exactly the same way as regular entries. The only difference is that you usually do not enter any data into the data fields. To create a model, choose Edit/Input Models. In the Input Models dialogue box select New. Enter a name for the new input model and click OK. The program then switches to Edit mode. Create an empty entry (or enter data that is to appear in all or most of the data, for example, a client's name or the subject field). Once you have finished adding the fields to the input model, click the Save button to return to the Input Models dialogue box. Before you can use the new input model you need to activate it by clicking on the Activate button. Click OK to return to the View mode. Every entry added to the existing database (by selecting Edit/Add Entry) will now be based on the input model that you just created and activated.

Importing terminological data

Most freelance translators, interpreters or other language professionals do not have enough time to build a terminological database from scratch. It is thus essential to know how to import data into your TMS.

We can distinguish between three kinds of terminological data that can be imported:

- terminology that already exists as digital data, because the user has managed the data using a word-processor;

- terminology that is offered by commercial suppliers as electronic dictionaries or glossaries on a floppy disk;
- terminology from online mainframe databases.

The following section describes how existing data can be imported into a
MultiTerm database. As you will see, a number of preparatory tasks must be
performed to ensure that the data is imported properly.

Importing data from a word-processor

Many translators still manage their terminology using word-processing applications such as WinWord or Word Perfect. When you move to a database manager
these existing collections need not be lost. Indeed, your database management
system must ensure that the existing data can be imported easily.

Before you actually import data from a word-processor into a MultiTerm
database, you have to follow a two-step preparatory process:

1. Define the database into which the data is to be imported.
2. Create the import file using a word-processing application.

In the import file each entry begins with two asterisks (**) on a line by themselves. This indicates the beginning of a new entry. Entry fields begin with a
field name enclosed in angled brackets, for instance <English> or <Definition>,
followed by a space. You can only use fields that are present in the database
you have previously defined. For example, if your database does not contain a
field named Definition but your import file shows such a field in angled brackets as described above, the import program will not find the corresponding field
in the database. As a result, the data will be attached to the previous field in the
database as normal text. It is thus essential to structure your database carefully
before you start importing data. Think about what language fields, additional
text fields and attribute fields you need. This will help you ensure that the
text file entry and the MultiTerm entry structure are congruent, and you will
avoid any loss of data. Further prerequisites for importing data from a word-
processor are that the contents of each field must not exceed 4,096 characters
and the complete entry must not exceed 32,000 characters. You also have to
make sure that the word-processing file containing the entries to be imported is
saved in either ASCII or ANSI format. Note that ASCII files have the extension
.tx8; ANSI files use .txt. The MultiTerm import program only accepts these two
types of file.

**
<Subject>Telecommunication
<Client>AT&T
<Project>ADSL ad
<English>network management
<Source>AT&T ADSL Manual 2/00
<Part of speech>noun
<Gender>
<Definition>Refers to the broad subject of managing computer networks. There exists a wide variety of software and hardware products that help network system administrators manage a network. Network management covers a wide area, including security, performance, reliability.
<Definition, source>PC Webopedia
<Context example or collocation>CMIS defines a system of network management information services.
<Context example source>PC Webopedia
<Synonym>network configuration
<Cross reference>network
<Spanish>gestión de red
<Source>diccionario de términos técnicos
<Part of speech>noun
<Gender>female
<Definition>Funciones relacionadas con la gestión de los recursos de la capa de enlace de datos y la capa física y sus estaciones a través de la red de datos soportada por el sistema híbrido de fibra óptica/coaxial.
<Definition, source>ITU, Termite
<Context example or collocation>
<Context example source>
<Cross reference>red
<Transfer comment>
<Note>

Figure 45. MultiTerm import structure

The actual import into MultiTerm is again a two-step process. First you specify the entries to be imported and the rules the import program should follow. Then you specify which file to import. After you have opened the database into which the entries are to be imported, choose Import from the File menu. The Import Options dialogue lets you specify what rules the import should follow, for instance which entries should be inserted, replaced or combined with existing entries. These rules are of particular importance if you want to expand or update your existing database entries. When you use a terminological database as a single user, choose Synchronize on Index Term and Add Entry As A New Term. The imported entry will be added as a new index term although the term already exists in the database.

Retrieving terminological data

Once you have created your database and filled it with terminological data, you can use it for specific needs such as a translation project you are working on. Regardless of the kind of project or work that has to be done, all terminological database systems have to meet at least one basic demand: they must be able to retrieve data in a quick and easy way. The search features offered by a TMS are thus essential. Here we will be using the sample database guidemo.mtw to show the various search features available.

MultiTerm offers various search options for retrieving terminological data. The simplest option is to enter your search term in the search field of the index dialogue.

Figure 46. MultiTerm's index dialogue

However, before doing this you should first select the desired source and target languages, using the corresponding drop-down list in the Index dialogue. Now you can enter your search term and press the Enter key. MultiTerm displays the search term in the entry window with all the information relating to it. If the search term is not present in the database, MultiTerm displays the next entry in alphabetical order.

You can also perform a global search using one or several wildcard characters. The asterisk (*) functions as a wildcard character (a special symbol that stands for one or more characters). This enables you to search for terms that have the same stem (for example, dialog*) or the same ending (*box). The search result, i.e. the matching entries, up to 50 at a time, are collected in a hit list.

MultiTerm also allows you to perform what is known as a 'fuzzy search'. When MultiTerm carries out a fuzzy search, it looks for all terms in the current index that have a certain similarity to the search criterion. The program then displays all the matching entries in a hit list. MultiTerm can thus even find misspelled or mistyped words. To perform a fuzzy search, type '#' at the beginning of the search field, followed by the search criterion (e.g. the search for '#short cut' will also yield 'shortcut). Fuzzy searches will only be successful after you have created or updated the fuzzy index for the current database. To create or update a fuzzy index, choose Create Fuzzy Index from the File menu.

The search options described so far only relate to the current index field, i.e. to the current source term. If you want to search for a word or a sequence of words in a specific text field (or attribute field), such as a specific part of a definition, you have to perform further steps for your search.

The first step is to select the fields for your search. This process is called filter definition. To select the relevant fields choose Define Filter from the View

menu. Clicking the Add button calls up the Select Field or Field Group dialogue. This box lets you define your filter by selecting the fields you want to
search. Confirm your selection either by pressing the Enter key or by clicking
OK. This leads you back to the Filter Definition dialogue where you can enter
your search term in the Criterion field. Enclose the search word or phrase in
asterisks (*). If you do not do this, the results will only reflect field entries
matching your search word exactly, so for example a search for the word 'box'
in the field Definition would only bring back definitions containing only the
word 'box', and longer descriptions containing the string 'box' and other words
would be neglected.

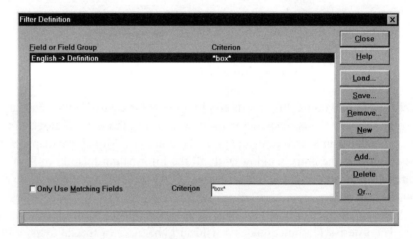

Figure 47. Filter definition

After you have closed this dialogue the filter must be activated in order to start
the search. To activate the filter you have to select the command Filter Active in
the View menu. All the entries that do not have the search term in the selected
fields are now displayed in grey. A hit list does not appear.

In addition to these options, the database can also be searched from within a
word-processing application (see below).

Exporting terminological data

Exporting data from an existing database may be necessary for a number of
reasons. The following sections describe some scenarios in which the export of
data may be of interest.

Backing up terminological data

As with any other application, it is essential to back up your databases on a regular basis. One option is to copy your database file to an external data medium. This may require enormous storage capacity. Alternatively, you can export your database entries into a text file, a process that is effectively the reverse of the import process as described above.

Creating word lists, glossaries or dictionaries

Although you are using a computer-based solution for managing your terminological data, you may wish to have a paper version of your data. This might be a word list or a glossary for a specific interpreting job, for instance. Publishing your language data as a dictionary could be another reason for choosing an export option.

Distributing terminological data

Since terminological data is one of the most significant 'raw materials' a language professional makes use of, it is usually guarded jealously. Nonetheless, there might be some occasions on which you need to forward or distribute your terminological data, for example if you are part of a team of translators collaborating on a large translation project.

MultiTerm offers predefined export definitions that you can either use as they are or adapt to your specific needs. You can also define your own export options from scratch.

The export of database entries from a MultiTerm database is carried out as follows:

1. Open the database that is to be exported partially or as a whole.
2. Choose Define Export from the File menu. This calls up the Export Definition dialogue that lets you either load a predefined export definition or specify user-defined export options. By clicking the Add button, for example, you can specify which fields should be exported. You can also decide whether the field names should be exported or not and whether certain text strings should appear before or after the exported entries or fields.
3. After you have completed your export definition, you can start the actual exporting process. Choose either Export This Entry or to Export All Entries (File menu). In both cases you have to specify a file into which the entry or entries are to be exported. If you want to export into an existing file, you are asked whether the existing file should be overwritten or whether the entries should be appended to the end of the file. To avoid the loss of existing data, you should choose the latter option. If no export file exists, MultiTerm automatically creates a new one.

We shall now look at some of the export definitions that come with

MultiTerm. To load an existing export definition, click Load in the Export Definition dialogue. This lets you choose an export definition either by entering its filename or by clicking on File and selecting the desired definition from a list of available definition files (all of which have the extension .mtx.):

- *backup.mtx* This definition causes all fields to be exported into a text file in MultiTerm format. This means the entries can be re-imported directly into a MultiTerm database. This export definition is mainly used for back-up purposes.
- *list.mtx* Exports a simple list of index terms.
- *tei.mtx* SGML export according to the suggested Text Encoding Initiative. This export definition enables you to use your MultiTerm entries with other database management systems.
- *rtf.mtx* Exports the data as dictionary entries into WinWord.
- *ventura.mtx* This export prepares data for dictionary publishing with Xerox Ventura Publisher.

Exporting data via WinWord

If you have the word-processing program WinWord installed on your system, MultiTerm offers further export options using three specific macro commands.

During installation MultiTerm adds a special template to WinWord called mt4win_e.dot. This template is designed for the simultaneous application of MultiTerm and WinWord 95/97/2000 (English versions, other language versions are also available). To create the glossaries and tables mentioned in the previous section, you first have to load the template into WinWord. This can be done by choosing New from the File menu and selecting mt4win_e.dot as the template to be used for the new document. You will find the templates in the Word folder of your MultiTerm '95 folder.

The template shows a new toolbar with MultiTerm-specific functions that will be discussed in greater detail in the next section. Three new options are also available on the Insert menu. These include the following commands:

- MultiTerm Glossary, which inserts a monolingual glossary, consisting of headwords and definitions, as a table into the current WinWord document;
- MultiTerm Print, which produces a complete dictionary, sorted by headwords, with definitions, translations and other information;
- MultiTerm Table, which inserts a three-column table containing headwords, synonyms and translations into the current WinWord document;
- Import All Entries, which imports all entries of the current database into the WinWord document;
- Import Current Entry, which imports the currently displayed entry into the WinWord document.

Exchanging data between a word-processor and MultiTerm

Dynamic data exchange (DDE) is a common standard in Windows. It allows data to be exchanged between two applications that are running simultaneously under a common interface. MultiTerm uses this standard to exchange information between a word-processing application and a MultiTerm database. This combines two essential tasks a translator performs, i.e. writing text and researching terminology.

Figure 48. MultiTerm icons in WinWord

The following routine tasks can be performed in MultiTerm using DDE (the symbols are named from left to right):

- *Lookup* looking up a term in the database and globally searching using wildcard characters (*)
- *Prev Entry, Next Entry* browsing through the database
- *Paste* inserting a target term from the database into the text document
- *Show Cur Field* displaying the content of the current field
- *Show Prev Field, Show Next Field* displaying the various fields of an entry
- *Popup* displaying the current entry.

All these functions are performed by macros included with MultiTerm. These macros are linked with the toolbar symbols supplied by the WinWord macro mt4win_e.dot (see above). The user can select these functions without quitting the word-processor. The results are displayed in the status bar.

The Lookup macro lets you search for a selected term in your database. If the term you searched for is not present in the database, the next term in alphabetical order is displayed in the status bar. By choosing the Paste macro you can insert the target term into your text document. The target term overwrites the selected search term. Note that the term adopts the font specified in the database. The target term may thus appear in a font different from the rest of the text.

If you want to see additional information on a translation you have found, you can use the Popup macro. This lets you place the MultiTerm window in the foreground so that you can easily read the desired information. By clicking the document window in the background you return to your current text document

The Show Next Field and Show Prev Field macros enable you to view information other than the index field. This allows you to insert definitions, acronyms or other database fields into your text document. However, you cannot restrict this to a specific part of a field's content since MultiTerm always pastes the complete field contents, e.g. a complete definition.

If you click the Lookup symbol without having selected a term in your text document, a dialogue appears that lets you enter a search term. If you specify a wildcard character (*) in the search term, MultiTerm collects the matching entries and places a hit list in the foreground when the search is complete.

The direct data exchange between MultiTerm and the word-processor enables translators to perform a terminology search while working on a text. This communication between a translation document and a terminological database can lead to an improvement not only in efficiency but also in quality.

Evaluating MultiTerm

Here we will try to assess the performance and capabilities of MultiTerm using the criteria expounded above.

1. Adding or editing database entries is a rather time-consuming activity. MultiTerm allows you to make use of input models to avoid building the database structure from scratch for each entry that is to be added. However, before you can add or edit an entry, you have to move from View mode into Edit mode. Here you have to open every single field before editing it and then close it again. This takes a great deal of time (especially if you are used to working with the mouse).
2. A solution to this problem might be to use the import function, which enables the user to input the data into a word-processor before it is imported into the database. This would avoid moving from one entry or field to the next over and over again. The import of external data into a MultiTerm database is carried out easily, thus also facilitating the conversion of terminology that already exists in electronic or digitized form.
3. The retrieval opportunities for terminological data are somewhat unsatisfactory. The search options are limited to the index field of the selected source language, which can be changed to another language as well. There is no real full-text search function. To search the text fields and attribute fields containing additional information on the headword is rather time-consuming and requires defining a filter first. Nevertheless, the user can easily perform a global search and a fuzzy search, the result being displayed in a user-friendly hit list.
4. The export options available in MultiTerm meet the demands of users wishing to export their terminological data for various purposes. MultiTerm provides the user with predefined export definitions that helps optimize exports.
5. The opportunities for communicating between MultiTerm and a word-processing application such as WinWord are exemplary. The integration of macro commands that are presented as additional symbols in a document template allows the user to perform interactive tasks between a MultiTerm

database and a text document. By combining the database search with word-processing and enabling the user to insert immediately a translation found in the database, the translation process may become more time-efficient and the output more consistent.

6. The integration of MultiTerm into Trados' translation memory application in Translator's Workbench is a definite plus. It allows you to use the terms collected in MultiTerm within the semi-automated translation process of the translation memories, thus considerably helping increase translation speed and terminological consistency.

Tasks

✓ List the various forms of computer-assisted terminology management and discuss their advantages and disadvantages.

✓ Name the criteria for the evaluation of terminology management systems.

✓ Build a glossary using a word-processor. Use the software's search feature to look for terms.

✓ Download the demo version of MuliTerm from Trados' website.

✓ Use the Guidemo.mtw file to explore the program features.

✓ Using MultiTerm, build a new database covering your working languages and areas of specialization.

Further reading and Internet links

Arntz, R. and H. Picht (1989) *Einführung in die Terminologiearbeit*, Hildesheim, Zürich, New York: Olms.

Austermühl, F. and M. Coners (forthcoming) *Computer-Assisted Terminology Management*, Manchester: St. Jerome.

Pearson, Jennifer (1998) *Terms in Context*, Amsterdam & Philadelphia: Benjamins.

Rey, Alain (1995) *Essays on Terminology Processing*, Amsterdam & Philadelphia: Benjamins.

Wright, Sue Ellen and Gerhard Budin (1997) *Handbook of Terminology Management. Vol. 1: Basic aspects of Terminology Management*, Amsterdam & Philadelphia: Benjamins.

Wright, Sue Ellen and Gerhard Budin (forthcoming) *Handbook of Terminology Management. Vol. 2*, Amsterdam & Philadelphia: Benjamins.

CATS: http://www.cats-term.de/
MultiTerm: http://www.trados.com
Termstar: http://www.star-ag.ch/

8. Corpora as translation tools

> *corpus* noun (pl. *corpora* or *corpuses*): a collection of written texts, especially the entire works of a particular author or a body of writing on a particular subject: *the Darwinian corpus*; a collection of written or spoken material in machine-readable form, assembled for the purpose of studying linguistic structures, frequencies, etc. (*New Oxford Dictionary* 1999)

As you can see in the above definition, a corpus constitutes the raw textual material for various forms of linguistic analysis. For example, by analyzing a corpus of documents written by a specific author, objective data can be gained about the use of certain words and phrases. The exact nature of a corpus depends on the results one is interested in. For instance, a lexicographer preparing a dictionary of teenagers' slang will put together a body of texts, mostly spoken language or scripts from Internet chat sessions. This corpus can then be used to identify the entries, words or phrases for the dictionary, along with examples of actual use. In a different scenario, French political scientists interested in finding out how much coverage their country gets in American newspapers (as opposed to other countries, perhaps) might turn to a corpus comprising American newspaper articles, perhaps as found on many CD-ROM-based newspaper archives. The political scientists would then start their search by counting the hits for certain keywords, such as France, Paris, Chirac or de Gaulle.

For translators, corpora offer a wide variety of uses. The most helpful is probably the chance to test one's own tentative translation (especially when translating into a foreign language) against the background of a large selection of original text written in the target language. Corpora can thus become powerful translation tools. Parallel corpora of source texts and translations can also play an important role in the formulation phase of a translation, in the field of translation memories (see Chapter 9), and indeed in the scholarly analysis of translation processes (see Baker 1996 and 1999).

The goals of this chapter are as follows:

- to explain what corpora are;
- to show the benefits of their use;
- to describe the different types of corpora available;
- to show how to use corpora in order to check the acceptability of word combinations;
- to show how to build and search *ad-hoc* corpora from WWW resources.

A typology of corpora

The different types of corpora are as numerous as their functions. In order to differentiate between them, we can refer to the following five categories:

- medium of original representation: oral vs. written
- medium of corpus representation: print vs. electronic
- number of languages: monolingual vs. multilingual
- characteristics of the selected text: regional, social, historical variations
- characteristics of the text preparation: annotated vs. plain text, statistical factors
- corpus functions: linguistics, philology, lexicography, translation, computational linguistics, information management.

We will now consider each of these categories in turn.

Medium of original text representation

The individual texts that will eventually make up a corpus may be in either spoken or written form. A spoken-language corpus will have to be transcribed in order to be analyzed (for an example, see the Wellington Corpus of Spoken New Zealand English, http://www.vuw.ac.nz/lals/wgtn_crps_spkn_NZE.htm). Contemporary technology makes it possible to digitize speech and to store the texts on computers in the form of audio files. An example of a corpus available in digitized form (in this case on CD-ROM) is the Corpus of Spoken Professional American English (http://www.athel.com/cspa.html). Speech-recognition technology might soon make it possible to analyze spoken-word corpora without the need for transcription.

Corpora consisting of written texts draw their data from printed or electronic documents or from a combination of both. Electronic and online publishing have created an enormous supply of electronic texts, and this has undoubtedly contributed to the rise of corpus linguistics.

Medium of corpus representation

Both written and spoken-language corpora are presented in written form. The medium of corpus representation can either be print or, more likely, in electronic form. The electronic representation of texts also allows for the integration of other media (specifically, audio and video). Thus, a corpus can also be used for the analysis not only of verbal communication but also for non-verbal communication. Such a multimedia corpus can be a valuable tool in the vast field of cross-cultural communication (an example of one can be found in Smith et al. 1998).

The fact that almost all corpora are nowadays available in electronic form (e-corpora) not only considerably speeds up the process of analyzing the data but also increases the accuracy and comprehensiveness of the analysis. A variety of software applications exist for the analysis of e-corpora.

Number of languages

With regard to the languages represented, we can make a distinction between monolingual corpora, which are composed of texts from only one language, and multilingual corpora, which are made up of texts derived from two or more languages. The most widely known monolingual corpus is the British National Corpus (BNC) at Oxford University (http://info.ox.ac.uk/bnc). The BNC website allows for online queries of the corpus (http://sara.natcorp.ox.ac.uk/) and contains a great number of texts on corpus linguistics in general.

As far as multilingual corpora are concerned, it is necessary to distinguish between those that deal with subjects and/or texts of a similar type, and 'parallel corpora', which consist of a given text and its translations in one or more languages. The history of parallel corpora is closely interconnected with the history of Bible translation, as can be seen in the Polyglot Bible project (http://mdavies.for.ilstu.edu/bible/). An example of a trilingual corpus is the French-Spanish-English corpus containing texts on telecommunications created by the Corpus Resources and Terminology Extraction (CRATER) project at the Lancaster University Centre for Computer Corpus Research on Language. The corpus is accessible via the Internet (http://www.comp.lancs.ac.uk/computing/research/ucrel/).

When a parallel corpus identifies which sentence and phrase of the target text is the translation of a given sentence and phrase in the source text, it is an 'aligned corpus'. The strategy of alignment is also widely used in translation memories, described in Chapter 9.

Characteristics of the selected texts

Most corpora try to cover specific aspects of language use. The text selection may thus be influenced by geographical, social and chronological criteria.

Geographic spread – International vs. regional
Depending on the geographic coverage of the corpus, one can distinguish between international and regional corpora. The International Corpus of English, for example, represents a selection of texts from 20 English-speaking countries and regions: Canada, the United States, the Caribbean, Great Britain, Ireland, Nigeria, Sierra Leone, Cameroon, Ghana, Kenya, Tanzania, Malawi, South Africa, India, Singapore, Hong Kong, the Philippines, Australia, New Zealand

and Fiji. Each sub-corpus consists of 1 million words, allowing extensive research on the regional varieties of English. Other corpora focus on specific regions, as does the Wellington Corpus of Spoken New Zealand English or the 1-million word Corpus of Estonian Written Texts compiled at the Department of Computational Linguistics at Tartu University (http://psych.ut.ee/gling/en/corpusb/).

Social and chronological focus

Many corpora represent the language use of a given social group (children, immigrants, men vs. women, etc.) or the language used in a particular historical context. With regard to their chronological spread, corpora can be diachronic, i.e. representing the development of a given language over a period of time, synchronic, i.e. targeting a defined period of time, or contemporary, i.e. reflecting the current state of language usage.

A good example of a corpus targeting a specific social group is the Bergen Corpus of London Teenage Language (http://www.hd.uib.no/colt/). Examples of diachronic corpora are the Brown-Frown corpus (American English from 1960 to 1990), the LOB-FLOB corpus covering the same period for British English, and the Helsinki corpus, which contains Old and Middle English texts. A synchronic/contemporary corpus presenting the current state of English usage is the Collins Cobuild Corpus, which is also used as the lexicographical basis for the Collins Cobuild dictionary. A sample of the corpus is accessible online (http://titania.cobuild.collins.co.uk/form.html). Any archive of current newspapers can be regarded a synchronic corpus.

Characteristics of the text preparation

Depending on whether the texts in a corpus are edited and marked for the purposes of analysis, one can distinguish between plain and annotated corpora. A plain text corpus, such as those provided by the Project Gutenberg (http://www.gutenberg.net/), consists of plain ASCII texts and does not contain any other information about the texts themselves. Annotated corpora, on the other hand, contain not only the textual information but also meta-information regarding, for example, formatting attributes (page and line breaks, font sizes and styles, etc.), the origin of the texts (data, author, source, etc.) and the grammatical structure of the texts, perhaps containing annotations for part of speech (PoS). This latter type of corpus is also referred to as a 'tagged' corpus, since the PoS annotations are called 'tagging'.

Corpus functions

The possible uses of corpora are manifold. Their purposes depend basically on the specific interests of their composers and/or users, although a single corpus, such as the Cobuild corpus, can be used by lexicographers for the creation of dictionaries or by translators to check the validity of a given English expression or phrase. An archive of scientific texts is a precious research tool for a scientist and also a valuable source of terminology for translators. Other areas of corpus usage include descriptive linguistics, computational linguistics and information management. See http://www.ling.lancs.ac.uk/monkey/ihe/linguistics/corpus4/ 4fra1.htm for more information on the possible functions of corpora.

Building and analyzing customized corpora

It is not always possible to find existing corpora that contain texts covering the specific area that a translator might specialize in. In this case a translator might want to put together their own customized corpus. Given the number of texts available in digital form, a fair-sized corpus can be compiled in quite a short period of time. The Internet in particular – itself a mega-corpus – can be a prime source of digital texts. In addition, many clients provide translators with a large amount of company and product-related text information in digital form.

Creating a corpus using Internet documents

Here we will see how you can build your own corpus by accessing documents available on the Internet. Refer to Chapter 4 to see how to ensure the quality of the documents used.

For the sake of this exercise, let us assume you are a translator specializing in technical work from English or German into Spanish. You are currently preparing for a large project in the field of telecommunications, let's say a project dealing with ISDN and mobile telephony. You will be looking for Spanish documents to download from the web for use as parallel texts (perhaps also as glossaries). The texts in your corpus should be of a general nature (introduction to telecommunications, ISDN, telephony, general dictionary or glossary of telecommunications terms), as well as specific (manuals for setting up ISDN lines, detailed descriptions of the working of the European GSM standard etc.). The contents of the websites can later be used as reference works to support your translation. All of this leads to a four-step approach:

1. Find relevant websites.
2. Download the files from this website.
3. Index the downloaded files.
4. Search the indexed files.

Since we are looking for a Spanish document within a given thematic framework, we might try a thematic search in Yahoo's Spanish site at http://

www.yahoo.es (or http://es.yahoo.com). In what category are you likely to find information on telecommunications? Try 'Internet y Ordenadores'. There you will find the entry 'Telecomunicaciones', and within the sub-category 'Telecomunicaciones' you will find a link to an 'Introducción a la RDSI' (RDSI stands for *red digital de servicios integrados*, the Spanish translation of 'integrated services digital network', ISDN). This link takes you to a rather lengthy introduction to the subject broken down into various chapters, with each chapter made up of one file.

Once you have found a website containing documents that you want to integrate into your corpus, you will have to download the files you need. There are two ways of doing this:

- downloading one document at a time;
- downloading all the documents of one website at a time.

If you want to download one specific webpage, you will need to make sure the graphic files or other files that might be embedded in the page are downloaded as well. If you just download the text portion of the page – which is exactly what will happen if you use the File/Save As command of your browser – you might lose valuable information contained in charts or tables. In addition, if you plan to download several pages that are part of the one website you might want to ensure that you keep the page's hyperlinks in order to use them locally as well.

The latest version of Microsoft's Internet Explorer supports the download of entire websites (Favorites/Add to Favorites/Make Available Offline); Netscape's Navigator does not (yet) allow for an automated download of complete sites. In order to download webpages with all the embedded files in Netscape, you have to open the webpage in the Composer (Choose File/Edit Page) and download it from within the Composer (File/Save As). Note that under Edit/Preferences/Composer/Publishing the options 'Maintain links' and 'Keep images with page' have to be activated.

To avoid the time-consuming task of downloading a site's webpages individually, you can use a special program that captures all the pages in one download. These programs are often referred to as 'web capturers'. Check http://download.cnet.com for a list of them (search for 'capture').

Retrieving data from your corpus with WordSmith

In order to analyze a corpus quickly and to find certain expressions, translators need to have access to software that enables them to retrieve data efficiently. This software is usually a text analysis program such as WordSmith, developed by Mike Scott.

WordSmith offers three tools for the analysis of texts:

- *Wordlist* A list of all the words occurring in the texts selected for analysis. The list can be sorted either alphabetically or by frequency. In addition, statistical information is available on word and sentence lengths, type-token ratios, etc.

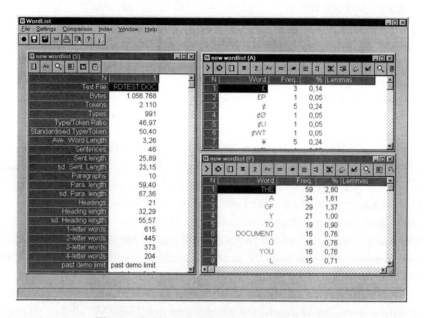

Figure 49. WordSmith – Word list results

- *Keywords* This tool allows you to compare a word list from a shorter article with the list from a larger text collection. This means you can find out which terms (keywords) from one list are 'most unusually frequent' in the short text. These keywords can then be used as indicators of the text's content.
- *Concord* A concordance shows the occurrence of a given search term in its textual context (i.e. the words to its right and left).

A demo version of WordSmith can be downloaded at http://www.oup.com/elt/catalogue/Multimedia/WordSmithTools3.0. The single tools can be selected from the Tools menu in WordSmith's starting window. To create a word list or a concordance in WordSmith you must first select the texts you want to analyze. Click Settings/Choose Text to start the selection process. Choose the files you want to add to the collection by selecting them and clicking on the Store button. Once you have finished the selection click on OK.

To create a word list, you now simply click on the start symbol or select

Start from the File menu. Click on 'Make a word list now' to run the analysis of the selected texts.

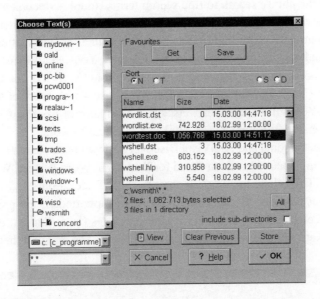

Figure 50. WordSmith – Text selection

To generate a concordance you must first tell the program what word(s) to look for. Click Settings/Search Word in the Concordance window.

Figure 51. WordSmith – Creating a concordance

Enter the search word and click on the Go Now! button to start the generation of the concordance. You can also create concordances of word combinations by adding context words to the word search. An asterisk (*) can be used as a wildcard (e.g. entering econom* would bring back the words economy, economics, eco-nomical, etc.).

Using AltaVista Personal to index and search local documents

In addition to 'classical' text analyzers, search technology used on the WWW can also be used for corpus analysis. Two utilities, AltaVista Personal 97 and

AltaVista Discovery, let you use the technology in AltaVista's WWW search engine to search documents on your local computer. You can use Boolean operators and the phrase search to find search terms stored in documents on your own computer. After you have installed AltaVista on your computer, the program automatically starts building an index of your files. Only after the files have been indexed can you use the search features. You can also customize the indexing process, thereby reducing it to specific folders, files or file types.

AltaVista Personal and AltaVista Discovery use a web browser to support the search. You will need either Netscape's Navigator or Microsoft's Internet Explorer (version 3 or higher) for AltaVista Personal to work.

AltaVista Personal and AltaVista Discovery allow you to search a variety of files, including documents from Word for Windows, Word Perfect, Word Start, Adobe or HTML files. In addition, spreadsheets (Excel, Lotus 1.2.3 etc.) and database files (Access, dBase, Paradox etc.) are supported, as are presentation formats (Freelance, PowerPoint etc.). Mail messages (from Eudora, Exchange, MS Mail, Netscape Messenger etc.) can also be indexed and searched.

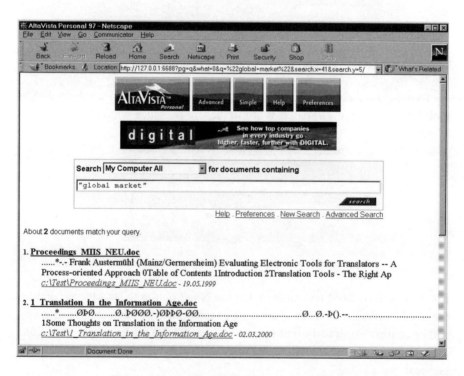

Figure 52. AltaVista Personal – Search results

Tasks

✓ What is a corpus? What is a bilingual corpus?
✓ List the different types of corpora.
✓ What role can corpora play in the field of translation?
✓ Perform a sample search with the Collins online corpus (see URL below).
✓ Build your own corpus using texts downloaded from the Internet.
✓ Build your own corpus using Word documents.
✓ Download WordSmith and analyze the Word corpus.

Further reading and Internet links

Baker, M. (1996) 'Corpus-based Translation Studies: The Challenges that Lie Ahead', in Harold Somers (ed.) *Terminology, LSP and Translation: Studies in Language Engineering in Honour of Juan C. Sager*, Amsterdam & Philadelphia: Benjamins.
----- (1999) 'The Role of Corpora in Investigating the Linguistic Behaviour of Professional Translators', *International Journal of Corpus Linguistics* 4(2): 281-298.
McEnery, T. and A. Wilson (1996) *Corpus Linguistics*, Edinburgh: Edinburgh University Press.

Bergen Corpus of London Teenage Language: http://www.hd.uib.no/colt/
British National Corpus: http://info.ox.ac.uk/bnc
Collins: http://titania.cobuild.collins.co.uk/form.html
Corpus of Estonian Written Texts: http://psych.ut.ee/gling/en/corpusb/
Corpus of Spoken Professional American English: http://www.athel.com/cspa.html
CRATER: http://www.comp.lancs.ac.uk/computing/research/ucrel/
Middle English Collection: http://www.hti.umich.edu/english/mideng/
Polyglot Bible: http://mdavies.for.ilstu.edu/bible/
Project Gutenberg: http://www.gutenberg.net/
Translational English Corpus (TEC): http://ceylon.ccl.umist.ac.uk/tec/
Wellington Corpus of Spoken New Zealand English, http://www.vuw.ac.nz/lals/wgtn_crps_spkn_NZE.htm
WordSmith demo: http://www1.oup.com/elt/catalogue/Multimedia/WordSmith Tools3.0

9. Déjà Vu? – Translation memories and localization tools [*]

Translation memory systems and software localization tools are designed to increase translation productivity by automating the linguistic transfer from source to target text. Unlike machine translation systems (see Chapter 10), they do not process a source text as a whole but work instead on segments. This chapter will explain the basic concepts behind these language technologies. We will show the operating procedures of two of the market-leading products, the translation memory system Translator's Workbench by Trados, and the localization tool Catalyst by Corel.

Free demo versions of both programs used in this chapter can be downloaded from the worldwide web. Translator's Workbench is available at Trados' website at http://www.trados.com. Click on Products / Free Downloads / Evaluation Software / Translator's Workbench and TagEditor. Catalyst can be downloaded from the website of Language Partners International at http://www. language partners.com. Click on Downloads / Trial Software Download / Catalyst Trial Download.

Translation memory systems

International companies require high-quality and 'high-speed' translations. But how can deadlines be met, time and cost-savings be achieved and quality be maintained at the same time? As far as the language industry is concerned, translation memories might be the key to this question.

Nowadays, the use of translation memory technology reaches far beyond the community of translators; it is also appreciated by many clients, as well as professionals in fields such as technical writing and software localization. This is mostly due to possible cost-savings and the need for consistency in style and terminology.

To fully understand the many advantages that translation memories offer, you first need basic knowledge of how they work.

Some things to think about

What does the term 'translation' memory indicate? Why would these programs be accepted and appreciated by translators as well as by their clients? Think of

---

[*] This chapter has been co-authored by Petra Dutz.

machine translation as a parallel example: It is certainly appreciated by many people who are not involved in translation, whereas professional translators seem to have taken a strong aversion to it. What might the difference be between machine translation and translation memories? How might translation memories differ from terminology management systems (see Chapter 7)?

What are translation memories?

Translation memories are part of the second level of Melby's translator's workstation model (see Chapter 1). They are databases that store translated texts together with the corresponding original texts. However, texts are not stored as wholes; they are stored in *translation units* or *segments*. In most cases, a translation unit corresponds to a sentence, although smaller segments such as table cell entries, list elements or even single words (e.g. a button on a dialogue box) can also be translation units.

Many texts, especially technical documents, contain numerous repetitive elements. Since many products are based on previously existing products, the corresponding documentation is also based on prior documentation. Research has shown that 50 percent or more of the elements in a text can be repeated in the same text (Spies 1995:3). If those elements have also been translated previously, it is obviously useful for translators to be able to recycle that prior work. With the help of search algorithms, the translation memory system compares the new text with the database and locates identical or similar translation units. It thus allows translators to retrieve the information stored in the database for use in the new translation. Translation memories thus recycle existing translations so as to reduce time and costs as well as improve quality and consistency.

How do translation memories work?

Translation memories (TMs) are usually built from scratch. This means you have to create your own translation memory step-by-step. The source-language text is entered as a whole and presented to the translator segment by segment; when the translation has been completed, the source and target are automatically saved as pairs. These texts then form the TM database. The more texts you translate, the bigger your database will become.

It is also possible to create a translation memory using existing translations. This requires the help of special 'alignment tools'. Using alignment tools such as Trados' WinAlign you can prepare source and target texts in such a way that they can be reused by the TM system. The alignment tool examines the source and target texts to determine which (sentence) pairs belong together. It then creates a file for re-use by the TM system. The alignment process can be based on several strategies, such as formatting information (e.g. style sheets or tags). The results can usually be modified and corrected by the user.

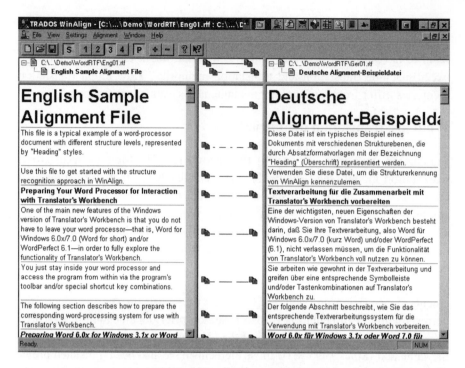

Figure 53. An example of aligned texts

As you are translating, the system continuously updates the database. When you have to translate a segment that is comparable to one that has already been translated, the translation memory recalls that previous segment and allows you either to reuse the previous translation or to modify it. However, fuzzy matching enables translation memories to find not only *identical* translation units but also *similar* ones. When using fuzzy matching, users can determine the degree of similarity that the TM must find before presenting a near match. Generally speaking, translation memories offer three categories of search results:

• *Perfect or exact match* The translation unit found in the database corresponds exactly to the new source text element (100 percent match).

Source	Target
(old): Nach intensiven Anstrengungen im Bereich der maschinellen Übersetzung wurde inzwischen erkannt, daß Translation Memory-Systeme heute das sinnvollste Hilfsmittel für professionelle Übersetzer sind.	(old): After intensive efforts in the area of machine translation, many have concluded that translation memory systems currently represent the most practical computer aid for translators.

(new): Nach intensiven Anstrengungen im Bereich der maschinellen Übersetzung wurde inzwischen erkannt, daß Translation Memory-Systeme heute das sinnvollste Hilfsmittel für professionelle Übersetzer sind. (100 percent match)	

- *Full match* The translation unit found in the database is identical to a stored translation unit with the exception of variable elements such as dates, numbers, time or measurements.

Source	Target
(old): Die TRADOS Translator's Workbench für Windows benötigt einen IBM kompatiblen PC mit einem <u>386</u> Prozessor, <u>8</u> Mb RAM und Windows <u>3.1</u> sowie MS Word 6.0 oder Word Perfect 6.1. Zu empfehlen ist ein Pentium-Prozessor, <u>16</u> Mb RAM und ein 17"-Bildschirm.	(old): TRADOS Translator's Workbench for Windows requires an IBM-compatible PC with a 386 processor, 8 Mb of RAM, Windows 3.1, and either Microsoft Word for Windows 6.0 or Word Perfect 6.1. Recommended is a Pentium processor, 16 Mb of RAM, and a 17" monitor.
(new): Die TRADOS Translator's Workbench für Windows benötigt einen IBM kompatiblen PC mit einem <u>486</u> Prozessor, <u>16</u> MB RAM und Windows <u>3.11</u> sowie MS Word 6.0 oder Word Perfect 6.1. Zu empfehlen ist ein Pentium-Prozessor, <u>32</u> MB RAM und ein 17"-Bildschirm.	

- *Fuzzy match* All other matches that do not match an existing segment exactly but range within a user-defined minimum match value (e.g. 75 percent) are called fuzzy matches. The sentence match with the highest degree of similarity is displayed first. All other matches with a lower degree of similarity are added to a match list which can be accessed by the user.

Source	Target
(old): The fuzzy matching technology used to find similar sentences has been re-designed in the new 32-bit version.	(old): Dabei wurde die Technologie des Fuzzy-Matching - also des Auffindens inhaltlich ähnlicher Sätze - in der Windows-Version erweitert.
(new): The fuzzy matching technology used to find similar sentences has been <u>extended</u> in the <u>Windows Version</u>. (79 percent match)	

If no match is found, the sentence has to be translated manually. The new translation is stored in the database and can, if the system's design allows it, be immediately retrieved for further translation.

Currently two types of translation memory system are available:

- *TMs that use a genuine database* This is the most common approach. Each translation unit is stored in a database that is available for further translations;
- TMs that use reference material: This approach makes use of previously translated texts that are not stored in a separate database. Instead, the user has to specify reference material (e.g. a previous version of the document to be translated) that will then be used as the basis for the *leverage*, i.e. the recycling of identical or similar material.

The currently available TM systems can also be categorized according to the way they handle new translations. Some TM systems can only leverage text; others are able to leverage and *propagate* text, propagating being the process of recycling duplicate material within the new text to be translated.

How to use translation memories

Some translation memories, including Trados' Translator's Workbench (TWB), have a built-in interface that works with common word-processors such as Word 97/2000 or Word Perfect. This means you can translate directly in the working environment you are accustomed to.

In such cases you do not have to import or export texts. Also, the format in which the translated text is stored in the translation memory is identical to that used in the word-processing program. Bold elements will thus remain in bold and italicized elements in italics, a feature that can be particularly useful for items such as product or company names.

Other TM tools, such as Star's Transit, come with their own editors. This means you have to translate in a different working environment; you have to import the text to be translated before you can actually start translating. Since most of these editors protect the original formatting by default, this information is also applied to the translation. However, unlike word processors, the editors make it much more difficult to modify the formatting information.

When to use translation memories

Although no computer program is currently able to replace human translators, high-quality tools can provide considerable benefits to the translation process. However, to select the appropriate tool, the workload and translation environment should be assessed in accordance with the following criteria:

- *Text type* What type of text is to be translated?
- *Re-usability* What is the degree of repetitive content?
- *Volume* How long is the text to be translated?

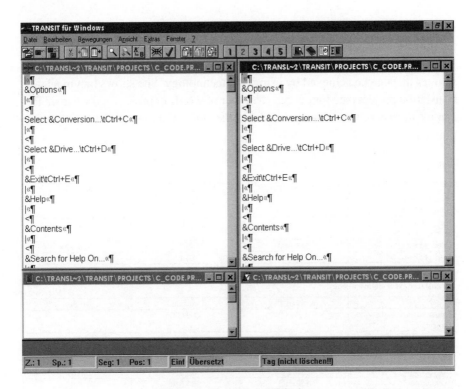

Figure 54. Transit for Windows

Translation memories are generally considered to be productivity-enhancing and cost-effective tools. Even so, some text types are more suitable for translation memories than others. The most suitable texts are technical documents such as user manuals, online help for software programs, lab reports and catalogues. Generally speaking, technical documents tend to be repetitive. This brings us to the second important factor in this context: the degree of repetitive content, both within the text (internal repetitions) as well as across several versions of a text (external repetitions). The more repetitive elements a text contains, the more suited it is for translation memory applications.

Text volume is the third key factor in deciding when to use a translation memory. The decision must be made on the basis of the initial cost of purchasing the tool and the potential savings that will be made when using the tool. Utilities like the Cost/Benefit Estimator (available at http://www. language partners.com) help determine the economic viability of using a translation memory tool. As a general rule, the longer the document, the greater the chance of repetition or re-use of similar sentences.

The benefits of using TMs

The benefits of using a TM can be significant, because TMs affect both the

quantity and the quality of translation. With a translation memory system, the
level of benefits is proportional to the degree of repetitions in the document.

A study by Lynn Webb (1998) illustrates quite clearly the time and cost-
savings that can be achieved by using TM technology. She shows that in a large
translation project (see Figure 55, 'Number of words in project'), the use of TM
can result in enormous savings, both for the client and the translator or translation agency:

Client

	Without TM	Using TM	Savings
Number of words in project	400,000	400,000	-
Number of days for turn-around	33	10	23
Total translation cost	$84,000	$50,400	$33,600
Cost per word	$0.21	$0.13	$0.08

Translator / translation agency

	Without TM	Using TM	Savings
Number of words in project	400,000	400,000	-
Number of days for turn-around	33	10	23
Total translation cost	$50,848	$15,784	$35,064
Cost per word	$0.13	$0.04	$0.09
Total profit	$33,152	$34,616	-

Figure 55. Benefits of TM technology in large translation projects (Webb 1998)

Other benefits of TM usage include:

- *Increase in income* Since translation with TM takes considerably less time
  (30 percent or 40 percent), a translator will be able to accept more projects
  within a given period of time (Webb 1998:12).
- *Elimination of repetitive translation tasks* Translator morale and product
  quality can be enhanced by letting a machine do the most repetitive and
  least interesting tasks of a translation project.
- *Consistency* The possibility of recycling existing translations certainly helps
  increase consistency, which in turn leads to an improvement in quality.
  However, 'mistranslations' are also subject to repetition and reproduction.
  In order to ensure that a TM has quality content, its database must be maintained. This involves removing errors from the source-text entries and
  target-text translations and updating terms that have changed. Unfortunately,
  database maintenance is often neglected. This is largely due to the fact that
  translators are paid less for the 'translation' of fuzzy and exact matches.
  The following prices may be charged when translating with TM:

Repetitions and 100 percent matches	25 percent of the price per word
99 percent – 95 percent	30 percent of the price per word
94 percent – 85 percent	60 percent of the price per word
84 percent and under	full price per word

What's the difference?

We might now ask which TM tool is the most effective: Translator's Workbench (Trados), Eurolang Optimizer (Sietec), Translation Manager (IBM), Déjà Vu (Atril) or Transit (Star)? The answer is: none. Some tools work better on specific file types than others, but none works best on all. Currently, no tool is available that handles all file types. Trados' Translator's Workbench, for instance, was initially designed to work with .rft files. Today it handles many other different file types, among them HTML, SGML and XML as well as several DTP formats. Star Transit is said to be a good solution for translating FrameMaker or Interleaf documents. Other tools such as Corel Catalyst were initially developed for the translation of software, i.e. resource files; today they also allow the translation of .rtf-based online help files.

If you are using Microsoft Word, Word Perfect or a DTP application, you will find that most translation memory systems support the respective file types. Most vendors offer additional filters for specific formats, and there is a strong tendency for TM developers to design TM tools that support a greater variety of file types. Since TM systems vary in their different functions, it is important that you evaluate them according to your specific requirements. Almost all vendors offer trial versions that can be used as a starting point for your personal evaluation. Once you have thoroughly examined the different tools, it is much easier to decide which to use in a specific situation.

Working with a translation memory tool:
Translator's Workbench (Trados)

We will now look at a typical translation workflow using TM. Generally speaking, the translation workflow with TM can be divided into three stages:

1. pre-translation tasks (preparation);
2. translation;
3. post-translation tasks.

Pre-translation tasks

Before the actual translation can start, preparatory tasks of analysis and defining TM options have to be carried out.

Analysis

As translation projects become ever larger, translation-project managers need to analyze the project to understand what savings can be made from the application of various tools. Most probably, both client and translator will want to optimize costs. Budget forecasting can be facilitated by an accurate analysis of the project. For this purpose, Translator's Workbench (TWB), like several other tools, comes with an integrated analysis function.

The analysis function is immediately accessible from TWB's toolbar (Tools/ Analyze). After defining the file(s) to be analysed, TWB carries out an analysis on the basis of a user-defined TM (see Figure 56). The calculated match values are displayed in a table for each file.

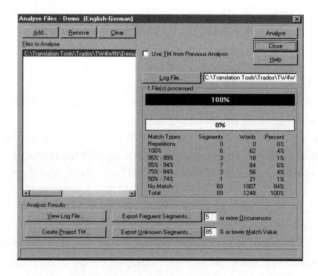

Figure 56. Analysis of project files

After analyzing the project files, you can create what is referred to as a project TM, which contains all the relevant data used for the analysis. It is also possible to export frequent or unknown segments for further processing, for example by a machine translation system.

This means that before a project actually starts, the analysis function makes it much easier to determine what kind of productivity gains the use of TM will bring.

Defining TM options

Before you can start translating, you must define the TM options. You can either create a new TM or use an existing one. For the following example let us suppose we will be using an existing TM as the basis for our translation.

First of all, start Translator's Workbench. Then choose Open from the File menu. A dialogue box appears in which you should double-click the translation memory you want to open, in this case DEMO.tmw. TWB then opens the respective file.

You may want to modify the translation memory options. If so, choose Translation Memory Options from the Options menu. A dialogue box appears giving you access to several tabs (Figure 57).

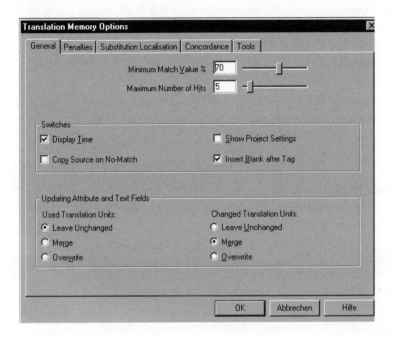

Figure 57. Selecting TM options

The General tab, for example, allows you to define the minimum match value. This determines how close the match between a given segment and any fuzzy translations in the database will be. Experience has shown that the minimum value should be set somewhere in the region of 65 percent to 75 percent. You can also define the maximum number of TM hits to be shown. The Penalties tab lets you define how matches from machine translation or alignment should be 'punished', i.e. how many points should be deducted if there are minor discrepancies (such as variations in punctuation or capitalization) between a segment and the corresponding fuzzy translations. In the Concordance tab you set the fuzziness level and several other options for concordance searching. Use the Tools tab to set various options for the batch utilities available in the Tools menu. The Substitution Localization tab allows you to specify how the format of variable elements (also called 'placeables' in Trados) such as dates, numbers or measurements should be adapted to the target language/culture. This feature can be particularly useful in software localization.

Specify all the options relevant for your translation project, then click OK.

Now, before you start translating, TWB offers another function that allows the 'pre-translation' of certain segments (Tools/Translate). This function can automatically translate all segments from one or more documents that reach a certain match value in the current TM. By default, TWB makes a backup copy of each file processed during the Translate function for later use. When you go through the text afterwards to translate it, TWB will present you with all the matches it has already found and inserted into your translation.

Translation

One of the most notable features of TWB is that you do not have to leave your word-processor in order to explore fully the capacities of the program. Instead, you can stay in your word-processor application and access TWB via the program's toolbar and special shortcut keys.

Start your word-processor and open the document(s) to be translated. Once you have opened the document, save it under a new name to indicate that it will be, say, the German translation of an English text. By now, your screen should more or less look like Figure 58.

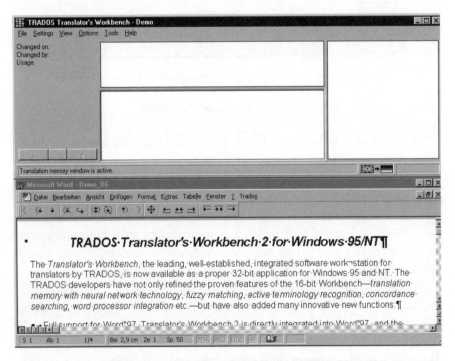

Figure 58. Working with TM and WinWord

Now activate your word-processor's program window and move the cursor to the beginning of the first segment to be translated, in this case 'TRADOS

Translator's Workbench 2…'. Click on the Open Get symbol ⟨↓ to open a new translation unit and (hopefully) 'get', i.e. find, a match for the current element in the translation memory. If a match is found, the result is displayed in TWB's translation memory window.

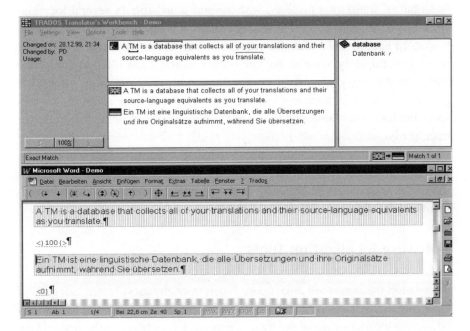

Figure 59. Presentation of TM matches

In this case, a 100 percent match has been found. To accept the translation without editing it just click on the Set Close / Open Get button ⟨↕ . This accepts and saves the translation, closes the current segment, opens the next one and tries to get a match from TM for this segment. If a fuzzy match is found, you can either accept the translation in the way described or modify it directly in your word-processor and then accept it. The translation memory is thus continuously updated and filled with new translations.

Additionally, if the Term Recognition option is activated, TWB displays all entries found in the terminology database MultiTerm, which is part of the software package (see Chapter 7). These entries appear in a separate terminology window, highlighted with a red line, in this case *database* with the German translation *Datenbank*. You can accept this translation by clicking the Get Current Term button ⟨↦ . You can now carry on as described above.

Post-translation tasks

The importance of post-translation tasks may vary according to the environment you are working in. As a freelance translator you will have to check your translation with regard to terminological and stylistic consistency before send-ing it to your client. You also have to check that possible changes and corrections are included in the TM.

However, post-translation tasks are probably of even greater importance in 'distributed' translation projects, with several translators in several locations working on the same project. In such scenarios, it is essential for the translation manager to check and update the respective translation memories on a regular basis. Unfortunately, none of the currently available tools offer an acceptable feature that entirely supports the co-ordination process. Although some tools provide functions for a terminology consistency check, there is not yet a corre-sponding tool that allows one to check the consistency of units that are larger than words.

Experience has shown that the use of translation memories can result in con-siderable productivity gains. In order to use translation memories effectively, though, it is necessary to begin by analyzing the individual working environ-ment and defining a workflow for each project.

Software localization tools

Translation memories are also a core function of the most recent category of CAT tools: software localization tools. Localization, often referred to as L10N (if you are wondering about the figure count the letters between the first and the last letter of the word), describes the process of adapting a product to the spe-cific situation of its target market. This includes not only translating the texts (and graphics) accompanying the product but also adapting to the cultural norms of the local market. Although localization is not restricted to software products, that is certainly an area in which there is a strong demand for the service of translators (or localizers). The tools used in the process of localizing software combine several translation-relevant functions in one application. Most of them offer, in one form or another, terminology extraction functions as well as glos-sary management features. They also provide dialogue box/menu editing in WYSIWYG mode (What You See Is What You Get), which allows translators to (re)view the localized elements immediately, as if using the application. Even if the main function of these tools is the translation/localization of user inter-faces (UI), some of them also include project management and software engineering features. One characteristic they have in common is the possibility of working directly on the files while the source code remains protected. Addi-tionally, most localization tools comprise pre-defined test routines that allow you to detect many common errors made during translation/localization such as, for example, duplicate hotkeys or invalid ampersand positions.

A localization case study – Corel Catalyst

In this section we will explain the main features of Corel Catalyst, which, along with several other applications such as Loc@le (Accent) or Passolo (Pass Engineering), is probably the most multi-faceted of the localization tools available today.

File types

Catalyst focuses on the translation of 32-bit applications for Windows 95 and NT, the most widely used operating systems in the PC world. Currently, Catalyst can handle the following file types:

Binaries/executable files	*.exe, *.dll, *.ocx, *.flt
Resource scripts	*.rc, *.rc2, *.dlg
Help Files (only available in the Standard Help Localization Environment (SKU 3) and in the Advanced Help Localization Environment (SKU 4).	*.cnt, *.hpj, *.rtf
Tabulated resource scripts	*.trs

Pseudo Translate Expert

Catalyst's Pseudo Translate Expert (PTE) lets you simulate the translation of the project files, thus allowing you to determine right at the beginning if the localization might cause problems. For example, PTE lets you simulate the expansion of a given text string (by up to 100 percent), which allows you to view how the user interface might be affected by differences in the length of source and target text.

Validate Expert

The Validate Expert is a quality-assurance function that allows localization errors to be identified automatically. Catalyst comes with a set of predefined tests for this purpose. For example, the Validate Expert performs tests for differences in the number of hotkeys (i.e. accelerator key which is used to activate a certain command by pressing it in combination with the ALT key) between source and target text, duplicated hotkeys in menus and dialogue boxes, mismatched empty strings, etc. The validation results are displayed in a separate window. Selecting a validation error immediately opens the object containing the error so that it can be corrected.

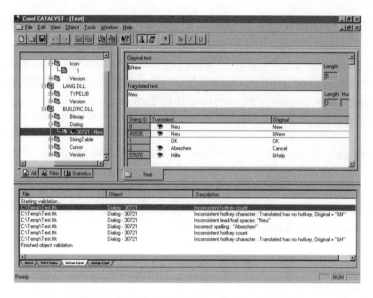

Figure 60. Identifying localization errors

Leverage Expert

The Leverage Expert is an integrated function of Catalyst's advanced versions.
It facilitates the re-use of translations from a previous version of a product. To
do this, Catalyst compares the new project with a previous one. Catalyst does
not create a database of all translations as, for example, Trados' Translator's
Workbench does. Instead, the user has to provide previously translated versions
as reference material. Catalyst then extracts identical or similar text strings according to the user-defined fuzzy match value (see above) and copies the
translations into the new project. The user can either choose to have this done
automatically or check each fuzzy match interactively. In addition to existing
projects, glossaries may also be used as reference material for a leverage. The
Leverage Expert also allows leveraging not only of text but also of dialogue
box co-ordinates (i.e. the size and position of a dialogue in the application at
runtime), thus reducing re-sizing tasks (i.e. those involving adapting the size
and/or position after translation). By re-using translations, the Leverage Expert
can help reduce localization time and ensure consistency among several versions of a product.

Project management function

Along with its translation and software engineering functions, Catalyst includes several project management functions that help simplify the co-ordination
of a project. For example, Catalyst offers the possibility of combining many

different files into one archive, thus making it easier to keep track of the single files. It also allows the sub-division of the entire project into smaller projects, which allows for distributed translation projects.

Another project management function is the History List, in which each major task is recorded. This helps to track the whole project.

Project monitoring is further facilitated by the possibility of generating word counts on different file types. Also, a statistical report can be generated to document the current project status. Since the report can be saved in .txt or .html format, it can be published on a project-specific intranet, for example.

Corel CATALYST - [AOLPress]

File View Object Tools Window Help

Object	Words	Translatable	Translated	Not Translated		For Review	Signed Off	Items	Sub Items
XNMTE455.DLL	0	0	0		0	0	0	2	
AOLPRESS.EXE									
PRESS	0	0	0		0	0	0	10	
Bitmap	0	0	0		0	0	0	2	
Menu									
XVT_WINDOWMENU	5	0	0		0	0	0		4
1000	59	57	0	(100%)	57	0	0		55
1053	281	281	0	(100%)	281	0	0		231
1276	131	131	0	(100%)	131	0	0		107
1381	30	30	0	(100%)	30	0	0		27
1406	6	6	0	(100%)	6	0	0		6
1413	82	82	0	(100%)	82	0	0		63
29510	37	0	0		0	0	0		25
29590	7	7	0	(100%)	7	0	0		4
Dialog	797	797	0	(100%)	797	0	0	47	571
StringTable	1597	1580	0	(100%)	1580	0	0	52	399
Accelerator	0	0	0		0	0	0	1	
10	0	0	0		0	0	0	614	
Cursor	0	0	0		0	0	0	16	
Icon	0	0	0		0	0	0	1	
XNMBA455.DLL	0	0	0		0	0	0	2	
XNMHB455.DLL	0	0	0		0	0	0	2	
XNMHN455.DLL	0	0	0		0	0	0	2	

All   Filter   Statistics

Ready   NUM

Figure 61. Word count report

Glossary management function

Catalyst allows two glossaries (in tab-delimited text format) to be attached to a project. When, during translation, Catalyst comes across a term that also appears in the glossary, this term is underlined in black. The translator then selects the desired translation from a drop-down list of suggested terms.

Catalyst allows for the extraction of terminology from previous projects, which can then be attached as a new glossary to the current project. This contributes to terminological consistency between versions. In addition, Catalyst supports the creation of a 'live glossary', which is made up of any translations in the project that is currently open.

Spellchecker

Catalyst comes with spellcheck dictionaries for 16 languages, among them German, French, American English and British English. You can also add words or even a list of terms to your own customized dictionary. You can either perform 'auto-checking', which looks for misspellings while you translate, or you can check the spelling after finishing the translation. When a misspelling is identified, Catalyst displays the word in a dialogue box and you can choose a correction from the suggestions listed or type in your own correction.

'No compile' function

Since Catalyst allows localization in binary files, you can generate a target binary file without needing to re-compile the resources. You can use the Extract Files command to extract files from the localization project and save them in their original file format (.exe, .dll, .ocx) (note, though, that Executable files can only be extracted in Windows NT). This extraction process enables the testing of localized executable files under Windows 95 or Windows NT.

Working with Corel Catalyst: translation of a user interface

We will now run through a brief overview of a typical translation workflow using Catalyst. To translate a Windows application using Catalyst, follow these steps.

1. Start Corel Catalyst.
2. Create a new project, then import the files to be translated. As soon as the files are imported, Catalyst displays their various elements in the Navigator window. Generally, you can use Catalyst to translate text strings, menus, dialogue boxes, version information and several custom resources.
3. However, if you have already translated a previous version of the product, you can first of all leverage (i.e. re-use) this translation with the help of Leverage Expert. For this, Catalyst provides several options. You can, for example, leverage from the same types of object (e.g. dialogue boxes only), leverage locking information from the previous version and/or use fuzzy matching. When using fuzzy matching, each match can be reviewed interactively.
4. Now you can start translating the resources manually. Just click on an object in the Navigator window and Catalyst automatically opens the appropriate editor in the Project window, e.g. the menu editor.

   Click in the field Translated text (non-WYSIWYG mode) or Text (in WYSIWYG mode) to enter a translation. If a term to be translated ap-

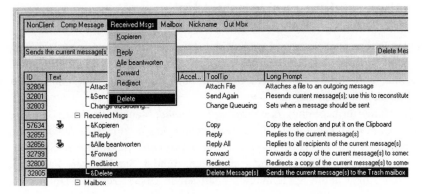

Figure 62. Manual translation of resource files

pears in the glossary, it is underlined in black. Press F2 to select the desired translation from a drop-down list of suggested terms.

5. Once the translation is complete, the project can be checked for localiza-
    tion errors. To run the Validate Expert, select Validate Expert from the Tools
    menu. In the Options tab you can select the several tests you want to run on
    the localized project, such as Inconsistent hotkey count, Invalid ampersand
    (&) position or Clipped text in dialogue boxes. Any problems encountered
    are reported in a separate window, the Results Bar. Double-clicking on a
    problem brings you directly to the respective object, which can then be ed-
    ited (i.e. corrected).
6. Once the validation process is finished, the files are ready to be extracted to
    their original format. To extract a file, highlight it in the Navigator window
    and select the Extract files command from the File menu. Now Catalyst saves
    the localized project file(s) and returns them to their original format. Note,
    though, that this function is only available in Windows NT.

Tasks

✓ Discuss the advantages and disadvantages of translation memory
  applications.
✓ What is the difference between an exact match and a full match?
✓ What is the difference between Trados' Translator's Workbench and tools
  such as Star Transit?
✓ Why do you think translation memories are particularly useful in software
  localization?
✓ Download the demo version of one of the translation memory and localization applications mentioned below.
✓ Use the sample files included in the demo versions to explore the program
  features.

Further reading and Internet links

Dohler, P. 'Facets of Software Localization', *Language Partners International*, http:// www. languagepartners.com/reference-center/whitepapers/l10nwp/triacom.htm.

Esselink, Bert (1998) *A Practical Guide to Software Localization*, Amsterdam & Philadelphia: Benjamins.

Sikló, Marie (forthcoming). *Localization Explained*, Manchester: St Jerome.

Spies, C. (1995) *Vergleichende Untersuchung von integrierten Übersetzungs-systemen mit Translation-memory-Komponente*. Saarbrücker Studien zu Sprachdatenverarbeitung und Übersetzen, Band 3. Saarbrücken: Fachbereich 8.6 – Angewandte Sprachwissenschaft sowie Übersetzen und Dolmetschen, Universität des Saarlands.

Sprung, R.C. (ed.) (2000) *Translating Into Success. Cutting-edge strategies for going multilingual in a global age*. American Translators Association Scholarly Monograph Series. Volume XI. Amsterdam & Philadelphia: Benjamins.

Tuthill, B. & D. Smallberg (1997) *Creating Worldwide Software: Solaris International Developer's Guide*, 2nd edition, Upper Saddle River: Prentice Hall.

Webb, Lynn (1998) *Advantages and Disadvantages of Translation Memory – A Cost / Benefit Analysis*, http://www.webbsnet.com/translation/thesis.html (20 Nov. 2000).

Accent (Loc@ale): http://www.accentsoft.com/

Atril (Déjà Vu): http://www.atril.com

Corel Catalyst: http://alchemysoftware.ie/

IBM (Translation Manager): http://www-4.ibm.com/software/ad/translat/tm/

Language Partners International: http://www.languagepartners.com

Passolo: http://www.passolo.com/

Star (Transit): http://www.star-ag.ch

Trados (Translator's Workbench): http://www.trados.com

10. A translator's sword of Damocles?
An introduction to machine translation[*]

Machine translation (MT) systems make up the third level of Melby's translator workstation (see Chapter 1). They are perhaps the electronic translation tools that attract the most public attention, especially among non-translators. At a time when expressions like the 'global village' or the 'information age' characterize the worldwide links in economics, politics and technology, a seamless flow of communication would appear to be a common ideal. Language barriers can, however, hinder this process. If product advertisements are to be believed, MT offers the perfect solution to this problem, particularly for companies operating on an international level. Here, for example, is what is claimed for one program:

> Need to communicate across borders? Globalink's new program helps remove language barriers. When you do business with international customers, Globalink Power Translator Pro 6.4 can let you truly speak their language. (Alwang 1998)

This chapter will present MT by showing not only its possibilities but also its limitations. We might then be able to assess the veracity of the many promises that are sometimes made for these tools.

Popular conceptions about machine translation

Public perceptions of MT often oscillate between two extreme positions (see Arnold et al. 1994:6ff).

1. MT is totally useless and a waste of time and money. The quality of output from an MT system is generally very low. That is what makes MT useless in practice. In this context often anecdotal episodes are cited as, for example, the one about a Russian MT system that translated *The spirit is willing, but the flesh is weak* into the Russian equivalent of *The vodka is good, but the steak is lousy.*
2. MT will bring down all language barriers, thus threatening the jobs of translators. In just a few years' time the translations done by machines will be as good as those done by humans.

---

[*] This chapter has been co-authored by Anke Kortenbruck.

The truth, of course, is that both conceptions are false. The wholly negative assessment reflects an underestimate of the possibilities of MT; the solely positive evaluation underestimates the limitations of MT. As is often the case, reality lies somewhere in the middle.

It is certainly not true that MT is useless in practice. Such claims are refuted by the fact that a number of MT systems are in daily use around the world. The 'spirit is willing' story is amusing but apocryphal. Variants of this example are quoted over and over again by MT opponents. Real MT howlers do exist, of course, but they are usually less spectacular and they certainly do not prove that MT is useless. As Arnold et al. argue:

> Seeing MT as a threat to translator jobs is also pointless. The quality of translations that is currently possible with MT is one reason why it is wrong to think of MT systems as dehumanizing monsters which will eliminate human translators or enslave them. It will not eliminate them, simply because the volume of translations to be performed is so huge, and constantly growing, and because of the limitations of current and foreseeable MT systems. (Arnold et al.1994:8)

Moreover, as we shall soon see, the professional use of MT includes certain strategies of quality improvement (such as pre-/post-editing and dictionary updating) for which a translator's human expertise is required. In this respect, MT offers translators new spheres of activity.

Machine translation and the roller coaster of history

The history of machine translation is marked by a significant number of ups and downs. This development may be described as follows:

Optimistic pioneer work

The first attempts to mechanize translation were made as early as the 1930s, although the Weaver Memorandum of 1949 is considered to be the first milestone in the history of MT. In his memorandum Weaver, the former vice-president of the Rockefeller Foundation, established a rather simplistic conception of MT by drawing an analogy between the process of translation and the process of decoding unknown signs, as was done for military purposes:

> I have a text in front of me which is written in Russian but I am going to pretend that it is really written in English and that it has been coded in some strange symbols. All I need to do is strip off the code in order to retrieve the information contained in the text. (cited in Arnold et al. 1994:13)

Weaver was convinced that MT was an entirely realizable goal and could be based on the underlying logic and universal features of language in general (see Schwanke 1991:70). His memorandum gave rise to considerable interest, and many research groups were founded in the US and Europe. In 1952 the first conference on MT was held at the Massachusetts Institute of Technology, and two years later there was the first public demonstration of a Russian-English machine translation system that had been developed at Georgetown University. Although the system was based on a very restricted lexicon of 250 entries and only six grammar rules, it was successful enough to induce further public financial support.

First-generation MT was generally marked by optimistic and even euphoric attitudes towards the new technology. Researchers in the field aimed at developing MT systems that could produce 'fully automatic high-quality translation' (FAHQT), i.e. systems capable of producing translations of a high quality, indistinguishable from those of human translators, without any form of human intervention. First-generation MT was primarily lexically oriented, while syntactic and especially semantic analysis of the source text played at best a minor role.

The ALPAC Report and its disillusioning impact

The first critical voices began to be heard at the beginning of the 1960s. In 1960 the US scientist Bar-Hillel criticized the concept of 'fully automatic high-quality translation' as being an unrealistic goal for MT research. In particular he pointed out that semantic ambiguity could only be solved by introducing vast amounts of encyclopedic knowledge. He thus recommended that MT should be considerably less ambitious in its aims.

As doubts about the potential of MT grew, in 1964 the funding authorities set up the Automatic Language Processing Advisory Committee (ALPAC) to report on MT research and the prospects of MT in general. The ALPAC Report made the following conclusions (see Schwanke 1991:73).

1. There is no need for MT systems as the demand for translation in general is not so high as to justify the use of MT technology.
2. MT is not likely to bring about fast and effective cost reductions.
3. There is no immediate prospect of MT producing useful translations of general texts without human interference. As Melby puts it:

> The ALPAC report evaluated the quality of the output of various MT systems and found it to be very poor [...]. The report noted that it was expensive to post-edit raw machine translation output in such a way that it became indistinguishable from human translation [...]. The report concluded that since there was no shortage of human translators and no cost

advantage in machine translation after fifteen years of hard work, there
was no justification for further government funding of machine translation for the purpose of developing commercial systems to compete directly
with human translators. (Melby 1995:30)

In view of what we now know about the constantly growing volume of texts to
be translated, the first point made by the ALPAC Report particularly seems
quite short-sighted. Although widely condemned as being narrow and biased,
the ALPAC Report had considerable influence on MT research in the 1960s. It
led to the virtual end of US government funding (see Arnold et al. 1994:14) and
most MT projects in the US were stopped. In the following decade, MT research took place outside the US, namely in Canada and Europe, where, in the
latter, demand for translation in the languages of the EC member countries was
steadily growing.

Upward trend in the 1970s and 1980s

MT research intensified in the 1970s, with expectations that tended to be more
realistic. It was generally acknowledged, for example, that MT should be used
only for certain kinds of texts, and especially not for literary texts. Using MT
for texts from restricted domains was increasingly considered to be advantageous. Accordingly, the first sub-language system was developed in Canada.
This system, which was given the name Météo, is still in use today for translating weather reports from English into French.

Elsewhere interest in MT was constantly rising. In 1976 the European Commission bought the MT system Systran, which had been developed for the US
Air Force a few years earlier. With up to 2,000 mechanically translated pages
per day (see http://europa.eu.int/comm/translation/de/brochure.htm), Systran is
still used extensively by the European Commission. In the late 1970s the European Commission also decided to fund an ambitious project to develop a
multilingual MT system for all EC languages, which came to be known by the
name EUROTRA. At the University of Texas in Austin, the development of the
Metal system was also begun. In the 1970s MT research work was mainly focused on the development of transfer-based systems (see below).

Apart from progress in research, the 1980s also saw the appearance of commercial MT systems, which were closely connected to the general increase in
translation volume in large public institutions and international corporations. On
the one hand, mainframe systems such as Metal or Logos were commercialized;
on the other, inexpensive PC-based systems began to swamp the market. The US
company Globalink Translation Systems, for example, started business in the
late 1980s by selling its main product, the PC-based system Power Translator

(see Lockwood, Leston, Lachal 1995:361).

Hutchins and Somers sum up the current position of MT as well as its prospects and future challenges as follows:

> There may still be many misconceptions about what has been achieved and what may be possible in the future, but the healthy state of MT is reflected in the multiplicity of system types and research designs which are now being explored, many undreamt of when MT was first proposed in the 1940s. Further advances in computer technology, in Artificial Intelligence and in theoretical linguistics suggest possible future lines of investigation [...], while different MT user profiles [...] lead to new designs. But the most fundamental problems of computer-based translation are concerned not with technology but with language, meaning, understanding, and the social and cultural differences of human communication. (Hutchins & Somers 1992:9)

Machine translation – definitions, architectures and quality demands

Here we will consider some definitions of MT and differentiate between the different forms of electronic aids for translators, including MT. The general architectures of MT systems will then be described and we will depict the different strategies for optimizing the quality of MT output. Finally, we will explore the relevance of special-language texts, especially technical texts, for MT.

Some basic terms

Hutchins and Somers give the following definition of MT:

> computerised systems responsible for the production of translations from one natural language to another, with or without human assistance. [...] [T]he central core of MT itself is the automation of the full translation process. (Hutchins & Somers 1992:3)

The degree of automation or — to put it the other way round, the degree of human involvement in the translation process — is expressed in the terms *fully automatic high-quality translation* (FAHQT), *fully automatic machine translation* (FAMT), *human-aided machine translation* (HAMT), *machine-aided human translation* (MAHT) and *traditional human translation*. Machine translation in the context of the above definition is involved in the first three terms.

As we have seen, the extremist concept of 'fully automatic high-quality translation' (FAHQT) was characteristic of the first period of MT development.

FAHQT, based on the idea that MT systems were capable of producing translations of a quality comparable to that of human translators, was soon abandoned. Nearly all MT systems currently in use rely on the assistance of human operators to achieve high-quality human-assisted machine translation (HAMT). In HAMT the source text is decoded and analyzed by the system, not by the human operator, whose task consists of assisting in the translation process.

Human involvement can take place either before, during or after the translation process. It may thus involve:

- pre-editing (preparation of the source text/input)
- interaction between system and human operator (interactive mode)
- post-editing (correction/revision of the target text/output).

If none of these possibilities is feasible, the result of the translation process is a 'raw' translation (unrevised) output from systems with no constrained or controlled input. This option for the practical use of MT systems is also called 'fully automatic machine translation' (FAMT). Circumstances in which this might be acceptable will be described below.

The term 'machine-aided human translation' (MAHT) includes the use of aids such as electronic dictionaries or translation memory systems. In contrast to HAMT and FAMT, the decoding and analysis of the source text lies in the hands of the translator.

The terms 'computer-assisted translation' or 'computer-aided translation' (CAT) are sometimes used to cover both HAMT and MAHT.

MT architectures

The 'architecture' of an MT system is the overall organization or abstract arrangement of its various processing modules. Most MT systems currently operating are based on one of the following:

- direct architecture
- transfer architecture
- interlingua architecture.

Here we will describe direct and transfer architecture in greater detail than interlingua architecture, since almost all commercial MT systems were or are still based on one of these two approaches. At present, interlingua architecture is mainly considered a research approach.

Direct architecture

> *Parsing*: Execution of procedures with the help of which a given charac-
> ter string is identified as a sentence of a specific language and is allocated
> a structure description (or several structure descriptions if the sentence
> is ambiguous). (Blatt et al. 1985:311)

Historically, the earliest approach was direct architecture, used in most MT systems of the first generation. In this context 'direct' means that there are no
intermediate stages in the translation process, so that the words of the source
text are more or less 'directly' replaced by their target-language equivalents.
This is done with the help of morphological information, bilingual dictionaries
and target-language reordering rules, all based on simple parsing procedures.

Hutchins and Somers (1992:72) illustrate the workings of MT systems based
on a direct Architecture, as shown in Figure 63.

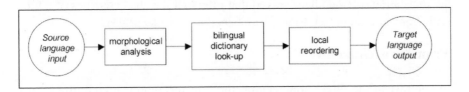

Figure 63. Direct MT architecture (Hutchins & Somers 1992)

The following features are characteristic of direct MT systems (see Arnold et
al. 1994:67f; Schwanke 1991:63; Schmidt 1998:133f):

- Since no complex linguistic theories or parsing strategies are implemented,
  the system does not carry out a complete analysis of the source-language
  sentence. Analysis of the source sentence is reduced to the minimum required for consulting the bilingual dictionary (e.g. identification of part
  of speech, singular/plural, tense).
- The system makes use of syntactic, semantic and lexical similarities between source and target languages, so the more similarities, the better the
  output quality.
- Direct MT systems are based on a single language pair, i.e. the information in the dictionaries and the implemented grammatical rules apply to a
  specific language pair. Adding a new language pair requires the development of an entirely new system.
- Direct MT systems are highly 'robust' in that they translate on the basis
  of incomplete information, as might be expected of commercial systems
  in general (see Schmidt 1998:133). Indeed, since they lack a linguistic
  foundation, direct MT systems characteristically have to make use of the

robust mode quite frequently. They thus even generate a translation when the source language sentence contains unknown grammatical structures or words, often leading to entirely unacceptable results.

- Since dictionaries are the most important components of direct MT systems, the quality of the output relies heavily on the quality of the dictionaries. The system designers thus usually try to allow for the integration of as much information as possible in the dictionary entries. This may be seen as an attempt to compensate for the system's lack of analytical capabilities. As Hutchins and Somers put it, "the paucity of structural analysis can be overcome only by the *ad-hoc* inclusion of multiple-word entries, resulting in a huge bilingual dictionary containing structural transfer rules hidden in lexical transfer rules" (1992:109).

The direct approach is becoming increasingly obsolete. The general tendency in MT research is currently to develop transfer systems. A good example of this development is the PC-based system Power Translator. Until the mid-1990s the Power Translator series was based on a direct architecture; now a generation of the translation software has evolved that offers all the characteristics of a full-scale transfer system (see Brace, Vasconcellos & Miller 1995).

Transfer architecture

In contrast to the direct architecture, the transfer approach comprises three separate stages:

- analysis
- transfer
- synthesis/generation.

The different stages can be illustrated as shown in Figure 64 (see Hutchins & Somers 1992:75).

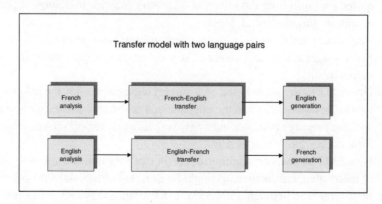

Figure 64. Transfer MT architecture

In the first stage, the source-language sentence is analyzed morphosyntacti-
cally using the source-language dictionary and grammar rules. The result is
represented as an abstract internal structure. In the following transfer stage the
abstract source structure is lexically and structurally transferred into an abstract
target-language structure. Only this intermediate stage contains bilingual rules.
During generation, the abstract target-language structure is transferred into a
target-language surface structure using a target-language dictionary and grammar.

The following features are characteristic of the transfer approach:

- Transfer systems are based on complete linguistic conceptions and theories, not only on individual grammatical or syntactic rules. They are thus
  superior to direct MT systems as far as translation quality is concerned.
- The analysis and generation components can be reused for further language
  pairs, provided the components are carefully separated (thus not containing
  bilingual rules) and representation is sufficiently abstract (see Schmidt
  1998:134). Due to the separation of the different modules, multilingual
  transfer systems can be developed.
- The dictionaries of transfer-based MT systems are also separate. There is a
  monolingual dictionary for source-text analysis (information for structural
  analysis and disambiguation), a bilingual dictionary for transfer, and a monolingual dictionary for the generation of the target text. In direct MT systems,
  on the other hand, all information is integrated into bilingual dictionaries.

Examples of PC-based MT software operating on a transfer basis include
T1, currently distributed by Lernout&Hauspie (see http://www.lhs.com/mt/T1),
and Linguatec's Personal Translator (see http://www.linguatec.de/products/
pt2000). As these systems are intended for general-purpose use, they also need
a robust mode that comes into operation when the source text cannot be analyzed fully. Most high-end systems, such as Logos and Metal, are also based on
a transfer architecture. This approach is generally seen as the most promising
one, particularly since interlingua architecture has proved difficult to implement.

Interlingua architecture

In contrast to the transfer approach, interlingua architecture comprises only two
stages, since the transfer stage is omitted. The source text is analysed into an
interlingual (language-independent) representation from which the target text
is directly generated.

The interlingua approach can be represented as in Figure 65 (see Hutchins
& Somers 1992:74).

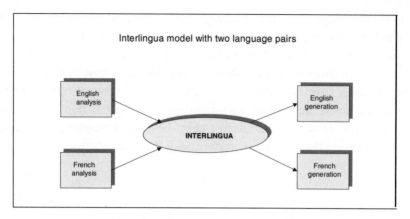

Figure 65. Interlingua MT architecture

The advantage of this approach is that the interlingual representation can be used for any language, so there is no need to use language-dependent transfer modules any more. Nevertheless, the transfer approach is often preferred to the interlingua method for two reasons:

- It is difficult to devise truly language-independent representations (free of elements depending on the source or target language).
- The analysis and generation grammars are complex owing to the fact that the representations are far removed from the characteristic features of source and target language.

In cooperation with the Carnegie Mellon University, the US company Caterpillar has been using an MT system based on an interlingua approach (see Lockwood, Leston, Lachal 1995:96,195; Lockwood 2000), but this approach is generally still of more interest to research than to practical use.

We now turn to the quality demands made of MT output.

Strategies for optimizing the quality of MT output

To assess the performance of MT systems we must first acknowledge that the ideal of FAHQT cannot be achieved using today's technology. The user is nevertheless offered certain ways of improving the quality of MT output. The strategies for optimizing quality include:

- updating the system's dictionaries
- pre-editing (including controlled language)
- post-editing
- human–machine interaction (interactive mode).

Figure 66 shows an overview of the times at which the various measures are taken.

Measure	Human involvement		
	before the translation process	during the translation process	after the translation process
Dictionary updating	X		
Pre-editing	X		
Controlled language	X		
Interactive mode		X	
Post-editing			X

Figure 66. Timing of optimizing strategies in MT

These measures do not exclude each other; they can be applied in addition to each other. Pre-editing and post-editing refer to the input or output texts, whereas the other measures influence the working of the program itself.

Strategies regarding input or output

Here we will look at strategies for optimizing the quality of a machine translation by working on the source and target texts.

Pre-editing
The quality of MT output is closely connected to how MT-friendly the input is. Pre-editing thus involves preparing a source text (input) in order to avoid problems from the outset. For example, to ensure that the PC-based system Power Translator Pro 6.4 can be used effectively, the distributor Lernout&Hauspie gives the following advice for preparing the English source text (see http://www.lhs.com/mt/text_eng.asp):

- avoid idiomatic expressions
- avoid omitting pronouns before a verb
- avoid omitting relative pronouns (e.g. that, who, whom)
- keep sentence structures clear, simple and direct; break up long sentences into shorter ones (one idea per sentence)
- keep to the typical word order *subject – verb – object* and avoid the passive voice
- avoid splitting separable English verbs (e.g. look up)
- keep to standard, formal English in which grammatical connections are clearly expressed.

This implies that problems can be expected if these 'writing rules' are ignored. In summary, the following phenomena are therefore likely to cause problems for the MT system:

- complex syntactic structures
- idioms
- ellipses.

Another point often mentioned with respect to pre-editing is the use of straightforward and perfectly clear expressions to avoid the problem of semantic ambiguity. Pre-editing also involves the identification of text that is to remain untranslated (e.g. proper names, addresses).

Controlled language and special languages

Controlled language can be defined as "a form of language usage restricted by grammar and vocabulary rules" (Arnold et al. 1994:156). It is in fact an extensive form of pre-editing, even though the concept of controlled language was not specifically developed for MT.

Technical writers sometimes have a negative attitude toward controlled language, since they feel it restricts their creativity. Multinationals such as the Swedish telecommunications company Ericsson, the US manufacturer of construction machinery Caterpillar or the British company Perkins Engines nevertheless make use of controlled language to enhance the readability of their product documentation. The 'Controlled English Rules' that the technical authors at Ericsson have to respect, for example, include the instruction that one word is to be assigned only one meaning, that each word is to be used in only one word class, and that complex syntactic structures such as conditional clauses are to be avoided (see Schwanke 1991:43f). Not surprisingly, source texts written in controlled languages usually produce better results with MT than texts written in uncontrolled languages. Nevertheless, even if the source text has been pre-edited or written in a controlled language, the target text has to be post-edited in order to achieve a high-quality translation.

A more general form of restrained input might be the 'special languages' used in particular technical fields. Such languages are characterized by carefully defined lexical items and by the fact that certain syntactic structures are used more frequently than others — in technical manuals, for example, instructional forms are predominant. This means that the MT system can be adapted to those structures. System designers make use of such advantages when developing sub-language systems adapted to "a particular syntax, semantics, and pragmatics within a well-defined domain" (Melby 1995:39). The best-known example of this is the Météo system used in Canada for the translation of weather bulletins.

General-purpose MT systems such as the Power Translator have been developed for general use and are thus not adapted to any specific language. Nevertheless these systems can also benefit from the fact that special-language texts tend to be less ambiguous than general-language texts.

Note that machine translation is mostly used for technical texts, especially in a commercial setting. This was confirmed in Vasconcellos' 1993 survey of MT users, where one-third stated they were using MT exclusively for the translation of technical manuals.

Post-editing

Post-editing is carried out after the translation process, as the name indicates. It refers to the correction of the target text, i.e. the raw translation generated by the MT system. Whether post-editing is conducted, and to what extent, largely depends on the quality required by the user.

Wilss (1988:183) argues that the tasks of pre-editing and post-editing should be put in the hands of professional translators who are aware of the limitations of MT, since without such professional intervention the process is very time-consuming and inefficient.

Strategies regarding the performance of the system

The performance of an MT system can be improved either by updating the system's dictionaries (before translation) or by interacting with the system (during translation).

Updating the system's dictionaries

The user of an MT system may adapt the dictionary component to their particular needs. This involves making additions, i.e. entering missing terminological expressions from the user's field, or modifying existing entries.

If the entry structure of the dictionaries is sufficiently complex, entries can be provided with morphological, semantic and phraseological information. Linguistic knowledge can be integrated into the program, possibly leading to better translation results. The complexity of the dictionary component should thus be taken into account when evaluating an MT system. However, one must also bear in mind that the complexity of the entry structure is directly connected to the demands made on the user: the more complex the structure, the greater the demands.

Human–machine interaction (interactive mode)

Some MT systems have an interactive mode that enables the program to consult the user when it encounters problems it cannot solve on its own. The system pauses during the translation process, for example when it cannot resolve syntactic or semantic ambiguities in source text analysis or when it cannot decide on one target language equivalent or the other. This means that errors can be avoided in the analysis stage. Different forms of human-machine interaction have been developed, including interactive modes for monolingual users who use either the source language or the target language only.

Quality demands

It is up to the user to define the quality required of MT. Whether and to what
extent the above strategies are adopted largely depends on these quality standards. If the user's aim is to achieve a translation indistinguishable from that
of a human translator, post-editing is of essential importance. Even if all the
other measures are taken (pre-editing, controlled language, dictionary updating, human–machine interaction), the result will still be no more than a raw
translation.

As far as strategies for optimizing MT output are concerned, the definition
of the user's quality demands is of fundamental importance. There are two standard positions: information-only quality and professional quality.

Information-only quality

Some MT output is "intended for information-only skimming by experts able to
visualize the context and discount errors" (Gross 1992:98). If information-only
quality is demanded, raw MT output with no or little post-editing is sufficient.
This low-quality demand is fulfilled when the translation is readable and com-
prehensible. Grammatical errors and clumsy styles are accepted, provided the
message of the target text is clear. The raw translation may also help the user
decide whether the text is relevant enough to be passed on to a human translator.

A well-known example of this is the use of low-quality MT output by the
US Air Force. Here the MT system Systran is used to translate scientific articles
mostly from Russian into English. Although the translation is by no means perfect it can help the scientists get a rough idea of whether the text is relevant for
them. Melby (1995:37) calls this 'indicative translation'. It is a market served
by low-end systems that explicitly address non-translators.

Professional quality

Pre-editing is of essential importance when the user requires target-text quality
comparable to the work of a human translator, as is the case with texts intended
for publication or for other broad dissemination, such as product documentation or marketing texts. How much post-editing is required in order to yield
'full-dress translations' (Gross 1992:98) largely depends on the quality of the
raw translation. As will be described below, professional quality is often as-
pired to when (high-end) MT software is used, for example in multinational
companies for the translation of product documentation. In most cases professional translators are employed to do the post-editing work.

The practical use of MT technology – high-end versus low-end systems

To give an overview of the MT market, we will compare high-end and low-end systems and their typical application environments.

MT systems can roughly be divided into high-end systems, which run on a mainframe or workstation, and low-end systems, which are installed on a PC. Examples of the first group include Logos and Metal, whereas the best-known representatives of the second group are perhaps T1 (Lernout&Hauspie), Personal Translator (Linguatec) and Power Translator (formerly Globalink, now Lernout&Hauspie).

One of the most obvious differences between high-end and low-end systems is the price. At least US$25,000 has to be paid for a high-end system. It is difficult to quote exact numbers here since these systems are mostly tailored to the needs of the specific user. The low-end systems are substantially cheaper, starting at around US$150 for the programs mentioned above. The professional version of the Power Translator Pro (7) currently costs about US$149 (http://www.lhs.com/store/trans.cfm). The Power Translator also shows that prices for low-end systems have dropped considerably in recent years. In 1994, for example, its professional version sold for around US$1,000.

Mainframe and PC-based systems differ not only in terms of price, but also with regard to their target groups and targeted application environments. High-end systems tend to be used in multinational companies and international organizations.

The use of high-end systems

Two representative examples of high-end MT users will be described here in more detail: the German software company SAP and the Swedish telecommunications company Ericsson.

SAP uses the mainframe-based Metal system quite extensively for translations from German to English. This includes the translation of software text strings, user manuals, training materials and internal reports. However, the system is not used for the translation of marketing texts such as press releases, which require stylized writing (Lockwood, Leston, Lachal 1995:234). The company believes that the translation of technical texts, particularly user manuals, can be done quite effectively using MT, since style is not as a high priority in such texts.

The Metal system is seen as a valuable aid for human translators, not as a replacement. Indeed, it is only used by professional translators. Part of the company's in-house translation department is responsible for post-editing MT output.

The post-editing is done to two different standards depending on the purpose of the translation. For texts that are intended solely for internal use, rapid post-editing is sufficient. Texts that are intended for publication, including all customer-relevant documentation, are fully post-edited and revised (publication quality). Further, the terminology held in the MT database is regularly updated.

SAP sees MT as enhancing productivity and of growing importance in the company's translation methodology. Since the company must bring its products to market as quickly and efficiently as possible, MT is seen as a useful aid for translators, enabling them to increase their productivity substantially:

> Using MT, SAP has been able to produce a 100-page manual in seven person days, including printing. The company has found that using MT, under the best circumstances, can be two to four times faster than traditional translation methods. An MT translator achieves an average of 15 pages per day, including coding of new words, post-editing, formatting, and feedback to the authors. (Lockwood, Leston, Lachal 1995:236)

This is also the case with Ericsson Language Services (ELS), a subsidiary of the Swedish telecommunications corporation Ericsson. ELS introduced the Logos system in 1992, hoping to achieve an increase in productivity of up to 50 percent for the translation of technical documentation from English to French, Spanish and German. In a project called Docware, ELS uses controlled language to improve the overall readability and quality of documentation. Texts written in the controlled language have also proved advantageous for MT, since further pre-editing becomes superfluous. To obtain a document of publishable quality, the MT output is post-edited – a task that is carried out by three professional translators at ELS (see Brace, Vasconcellos, Miller 1995).

The features common to these two examples are characteristic of the professional and extensive use of high-end systems. They can be summarized as follows:

- *Target group* Business users, 'industrial strength users' (Vasconcellos 1993) or international institutions and organizations (e.g. the use of Systran in the EU translation service) benefit most from high-end systems;
- *Processing of huge translation volumes (increase in productivity)* A certain minimum translation volume has to be reached to justify the investment in an high-end MT system: "The break point that appears to justify using MT is an output per language combination of at least 1,000,000 words (4,000 pages) of translation per year" (Brace, Vasconcellos, Miller 1995);
- *Genre* The texts translated are mainly technical, e.g. product documentation;
- *Role* MT is an aid to (not a replacement of) professional translators;

- *Extent of pre-editing and/or post-editing of the MT output or controlled language* The extent of the post-editing depends on the purpose of the translation;
- *Updating* The systems' dictionaries are updated (user-specific terminology).

In this context the OVUM report uses the expression 'Production MT' to characterize "large, multi-user systems for high-volume translation environments" (Lockwood, Leston, Lachal 1995:92).

The use of low-end systems

The market for PC-based MT systems is booming. In the 1990s sales figures increased considerably as a growing number of suppliers of high-end systems started selling low-end variants of their products. T1, to name one, is a low-end version based on the Metal system. These low-end, PC-based systems enable machine translation to reach larger user groups. Their relatively low price (as low as US$39) means that PC-based systems address not professional translators or industrial users, but non-translators or casual users.

The main use of low-end MT software can be described as occasional translation for information-only purposes (indicative translation). PC-based systems thus also address monolingual users who know only the target language. Such users are interested in interpreting the content of texts that would otherwise remain inaccessible to them. PC-based systems thus explicitly aim at the 'low-quality market'.

Examples of occasional translations for information-only purposes include the automatic translation of webpages. The importance of this application environment can be seen from the fact that some PC-based systems such as the Power Translator Pro offer a supplementary module for the translation of HTML documents. Several MT services are also available directly on the Internet. The search engine AltaVista, for example, offers the possibility of having its search results directly translated using the MT system Systran. We will soon have a closer look at some of the MT Internet systems.

A further development in the Internet market is the use of MT-based client-server systems. The Belgian speech-technology company Lernout&Hauspie, which has acquired several MT engines (T1, Power Translator), offers the client-server product iTranslator. This software enables a file to be sent to the server on which the various translation engines are available. The server then returns the translation in the chosen language (see http://www.lhs.com/ itranslator). Lernout&Hauspie also offers a 'premium translation service' with human post-editing or proof-reading.

Many suppliers of PC-based MT systems also offer professional versions of their systems, thus attempting to address the business market as well. The occasional use of PC-based systems by non-translators in a non-business environment nevertheless remains the more typical application environment.

The use of low-end systems (in contrast to high-end systems) can be summarized as follows:

- *Target group* Mainly non-translators or casual users (even monolingual users);
- *Purpose* The main application is translation for information-only purposes (indicative translation);
- *Restrictions* No restrictions concerning text types;
- *Volume* Occasional translation, in contrast to high-volume use;
- *Environment* Use in a private rather than business environment;
- *Pre-editing and post-editing* These are of minor importance;
- *Market* Translation for the low-quality market.

For these 'stand-alone desktop products for casual translation needs' the OVUM report coined the expression 'Personal MT' (Lockwood, Leston, Lachal 1995:92). The prospects for PC-based MT software are generally considered rosy. So what does the future of MT look like? Well, it runs on a PC and it costs less than US$500 (see Brace, Vasconcellos, Miller 1995).

Notorious problems in MT

In this section we will describe just a few of the common sources of notorious problems in MT, as well as the strategies commonly applied to solve them. It is useful to categorize the problems under four headings:

- ambiguity
- syntactic complexity
- idioms
- anaphora resolution.

Ambiguity

Ambiguity is a pervasive phenomenon in human languages. There are numerous forms of ambiguity. A rough distinction may nevertheless be made between lexical and structural ambiguity.

Lexical ambiguity occurs when one word can mean more than one thing. Central phenomena in this context are polysemy and homography (when a word can belong to different grammatical categories). A well-known example is the word *round* in the following sentences (see Hutchins & Somers 1992:85):

a) Liverpool was eliminated in the first *round*. (noun)

b) The cowboy started to *round* up the cattle. (verb)
c) I want to buy a *round* table. (adjective)
d) We are going on a cruise *round* the world. (preposition)
e) A bucket of cold water soon brought him *round*. (particle)
f) The tree measured six feet *round*. (adverb)

Homographs can often be rendered unambiguous by syntactic parsing. *Round* in sentence (b) can only be analyzed as a verb, because the syntactic context determines that only a verb would be appropriate. The problems increase when the syntactic structure of the sentence is complex or incomplete. Headlines are thus often difficult for MT systems. For example, the translation of the section title 'Gerät öffnen' by Power Translator Pro 6.4 reads 'Gets opens' (instead of something like 'Open device' or 'Open machine'). *Gerät* was clearly misinterpreted as a verb (*geraten*, to get). Generally, however, the disambiguation of homographs is more straightforward than that of polysemes.

Polysemes are two or more words that belong to the same grammatical category but can be assigned different meanings, for example *bank* (financial institution vs. riverside), *light* (not dark vs. not heavy). In MT polysemes become relevant when the translation of the word in question varies according to meaning (e.g. *light* as *bright* or *without substantial weight*). Syntactic analysis is not much use in the disambiguation of polysemes. Instead, the definition of a subject field may prove useful. The noun *bank* in a text about the English economy is more likely to refer to a financial institution than to a riverside. So the more unusual usage is simply excluded from the dictionary unless it is appropriate to the subject field of the source text.

Another common approach to the disambiguation of polysemes is the use of semantic information in assigning features such as 'female', 'human' or 'liquid', and to specify which features are compatible in given syntactic constructions via selection restrictions. It might be specified, for example, that the verb *drink* must have an animate subject. This approach is widely used in MT systems. Yet it is not as straightforward as it might seem. It is quite difficult to devise a consistently applicable set of semantic features and to specify the selection restrictions of nouns and verbs in terms of such features. Linguistic knowledge alone is often not enough. To disambiguate Bar-Hillel's famous example 'The box is in the pen', the world knowledge that *pen* must refer to a playpen or pigpen rather then a writing instrument is required. The introduction of such knowledge into an MT system has proved to be very difficult, if not impossible.

In contrast to lexical ambiguity, which refers to individual words, structural ambiguity has to do with syntactic structures and representations of sentences. Common examples are ambiguities resulting from the fact that whole phrases, typically prepositional phrases, can be attached to more than one position in a sentence. The following examples illustrate the problem:

a) The man saw the horse with the telescope (see Hutchins & Somers 1992:93).
b) Connect the printer to a word-processor package with a Postscript interface (see Arnold et al. 1994:114).

In both cases world knowledge is needed to disambiguate the sentence. In the second example, for instance, knowledge is required about what a Postscript printer is (i.e. a piece of software, not a piece of hardware that can be used for making a physical connection between a printer and a computer).

Syntactic complexity

Complex syntactic structures are common sources of mistakes during MT analysis. If the system fails to analyze the sentence completely and to assign the correct grammatical categories, it has to fall back on the robust mode, translating word-by-word and copying the structures of the source sentence. The following example, produced by the Power Translator Professional 5.0, illustrates the problem:

a) Schalten Sie einen ProPrint 100 am Schalter, der sich am PC befindet, aus.
b) Switch off a ProPrint 100 at the switch, which is situated at the PC, from.

In this sentence the embedded relative clause massively disturbs analysis (the system actually translates correctly when the relative clause is left out) since the connection between the verb (*schalten*) and its detached prefix (*aus*) cannot be established. Instead, the system generates a word-by-word translation that lacks grammaticality.

This example illustrates why pre-editing often involves simplifying complex syntactic structures.

Idioms

Idioms are "expressions whose meaning cannot be completely understood from the meanings of its components" (Arnold et al. 1994:122). This is precisely what makes idioms difficult for MT systems to handle. If the English idiom 'kick the bucket' is translated word-by-word into German, for example, the result is complete nonsense ('den Eimer treten'); a German reader could not guess the meaning of the idiom (i.e. to die). In MT systems, idioms have to be treated as single units of translation. This is often done by including them in the system's dictionaries. However, it is safer and less time-consuming to avoid the use of idioms altogether. Indeed, this is often cited as a principle of pre-editing. Luckily, idioms are relatively rare in the special-language texts that make up the majority of texts submitted to MT.

Anaphora resolution

Anaphora resolution is another major difficulty of MT. The term 'anaphora' is used in linguistics to refer to the use of a word that has the same reference as a previous word. The most frequent case is the use of pronouns. Resolving pronoun references requires the identification of the pronoun's antecedent, i.e. the noun to which the pronoun refers. This is especially important when translating into languages that mark the gender of the pronoun, as is the case with German. The following examples illustrate the problem (see Hutchins & Somers 1992:95):

   a) The monkey ate the banana because it was hungry.
   b) The monkey ate the banana because it was ripe.

In each sentence the pronoun *it* refers to something different: in the first sentence to the antecedent *monkey* and in the second sentence to *banana*. Since German pronouns take the same grammatical gender as their antecedents, the correct translation for *it* in the first sentence would be *er* (der Affe) and in the second sentence the appropriate pronoun would be *sie* (die Banane). In order to make the correct choice, the MT system must use linguistic knowledge. In the first sentence the system must 'know', for example, that *hungry* must refer to an animate subject. For some pronoun references, though, the use of linguistic knowledge alone is not sufficient. Consider the following sentences (see Arnold et al.1994:114):

   c) Put the paper in the printer. Then switch it on.

To get the pronoun references right, one requires the world knowledge that printers rather than paper are the sort of thing one is likely to switch on. As already mentioned, such world knowledge is particularly difficult to implement in MT systems.

Some systems even fail in obvious cases. Power Translator Pro 6.4 translates the sentence 'Schwenken Sie die Farbbandkassette nach hinten, bis sie einrastet' as follows: 'Wave then the ribbon-cassette to the back until she/it locks'. The system does not even attempt to carry out a proper analysis. Instead it simply offers all possible solutions leaving it to the user to select the right one. (If you don't know German, what would you do with the 'ribbon-cassette'?)

Since MT systems usually operate on the sentence level, the resolution of cross-sentence connections is generally impracticable using today's technology.

From the information presented in this section, one might conclude that designing an MT system requires the inclusion of vast amounts of knowledge. The limitations of MT systems are still profound and will remain so in the foreseeable future. This does not mean, however, that MT cannot be used effectively. If applied to a restricted domain of knowledge and used in addition to strategies for quality improvement, MT is a useful but labour-intensive aid for translators.

MT on the Internet

Here you will be able to see for yourself what MT output is like and come to your own conclusions about its usefulness. As mentioned above, several MT systems are available on the Internet for evaluation purposes. Examples include T1(http://t1.sail-labs.com/t1probe.html) andSystran (http:// www. systrans oft. com). Note that these do not allow the possibility of making additions to the system's dictionaries. The quality of the translation can thus be affected negatively by the fact that the source text may contain unknown words.

Try out the Internet MT programmes by submitting either a text of your own choice, the sentences given as examples above, or sentences from the sample text below. In the case of Systran you can also translate webpages by simply entering their URLs. Systran automatically translate the contents of the specified page, while keeping its original layout.

Note that for T1 it is only possible to enter one sentence at a time, so you may need to perform several 'test drives'. Further, the demo version only allows translations from German to English or from Spanish to English. The text below is taken from a user manual (Siemens Nixdorf Informationssysteme AG 1997:3f) as this kind of text type is often used in MT.

Sample text

> Geräteübersicht
> Wichtige Sicherheitshinweise

- Lesen Sie bitte vor Inbetriebnahme die folgenden Hinweise aufmerksam durch, und verwahren Sie diese Informationen zum späteren Nachschlagen.
- Dieses Gerät entspricht den einschlägigen Sicherheitsbestimmungen für Geräte der Informationstechnik und ist für den Einsatz in normaler Büroumgebung vorgesehen.
- Wird das Gerät aus kalter Umgebung in den Betriebsraum gebracht, kann Betauung auftreten.
- Vor Inbetriebnahme muß das Gerät absolut trocken sein, deshalb ist eine Akklimatisationszeit von mindestens zwei Stunden abzuwarten.
- Transportieren Sie das Gerät nur in der Originalverpackung.

- Überprüfen Sie, ob die eingestellte Nennspannung des Gerätes mit der örtlichen Netzspannung übereinstimmt.
- Dieses Gerät ist mit einer sicherheitsgeprüften Netzleitung ausgestattet. Schließen Sie es nur an eine geerdete Schutzkontaktsteckdose an.
- Verlegen Sie alle Leitungen so, daß niemand darauf treten oder darüber stolpern kann.
- Fassen Sie das Netzkabel beim Anschließen oder Abziehen immer am Stecker an. Ziehen Sie niemals am Kabel selbst.
- Sorgen Sie dafür, daß der Netzanschluß immer leicht zugänglich ist.
- Wechseln Sie ein beschädigtes Netzkabel sofort aus.
- Bei Wartungsarbeiten und der Behebung von Störungen müssen Sie vor dem Öffnen des Gerätes den Netzstecker ziehen.
- In Notfällen, z.B. wenn das Gehäuse, ein Bedienelement oder das Netzkabel beschädigt ist, oder wenn eine Flüssigkeit oder ein fester Gegenstand in das Gehäuseinnere geraten sein sollte, schalten Sie das Gerät aus und ziehen Sie sofort den Netzstecker.
- Lassen Sie das Gerät von einem autorisierten Fachmann überprüfen.
- Während eines Gewitters dürfen Datenübertragungsleitungen weder angeschlossen noch gelöst werden.
- Schützen Sie das Gerät vor direkter Sonnenbestrahlung, Staub, Vibration und Stößen.

Compare the results for the various MT systems. Are there any differences in quality? Can you detect any mistakes of the kind described above? What additional problems are there? Try to summarize them in different categories. What kinds of mistakes do you think are most striking? How do they affect the readability of the text? Does the fact that T1 allows the selection of a domain influence the translation results? Would you consider buying one of the systems as result of your test drives?

You might also try out the automatic translation of webpages provided by the search engine AltaVista (http://www.altavista.com). Under each search result the Translate button allows you to have the webpage automatically translated by Systran. Try out different kinds of webpages. What is your general impression? Do the results differ according to the type of webpage? Note that the overall purpose of this kind of machine translation is indicative translation (information-only quality). Do you think the results meet this kind of quality demand?

Tasks

✓ What is the ALPAC Report?
✓ Describe the kinds of human involvement that can take place in an MT process.

✓ Describe the different types of MT architecture.
✓ What are the benefits of a controlled language?
✓ What are the different stages of the transfer architecture?
✓ What is an interlingua?
✓ What strategies can be used to optimize the output of an MT system?

Further reading and Internet links

Arnold, D., L. Balken, L. Humphreys, S. Meijer, L. Sadler (eds) (1994) *Machine Translation. An Introductory Guide*, London: NCC Blackwell.
Brace, C., M. Vasconcellos, C. Miller (1995) *MT Users and Usage: Europe and the Americas*, http://www.lim.nl/eamt/archive/summit95.html (20 Nov. 2000).
Cole, R.A., J. Mariani, J. Uszkoreit, A. Zaenen, V. Zue, (1996) *Survey of the State of the Art in Human Language Technology*, http://cslu.cse.ogi.edu/HLTsurvey/ (20 Nov. 2000).
Hutchins, J. (1996) *Computer-based translation systems and tools*, http://www.lim.nl/eamt/archive/hutchins_intro.html (20 Nov. 2000).
Hutchins, J. and H. Somers (1992) *An Introduction to Machine Translation*, London: Academic Press.
Lockwood, R. (2000) 'Machine Translation and Controlled Authoring at Caterpillar' in: R. Sprung (ed.) *Translating Into Success. Cutting-edge strategies for going multilingual in a global age.* American Translators Association Scholarly Monograph Series. Volume XI. Amsterdam/Philadelphia: John Benjamins. 187-202.
Melby, Alan K. (1995) *The Possibility of Language*. Amsterdam & Philadelphia: Benjamins.

AltaVista: http://www.altavista.com
Lernout&Hauspie: http://www.lhs.com
Lernout&Hauspie: *L&H iTranslator*: http://www.lhs.com/itranslator.
Linguatec: http://www.linguatec.de/products/pt2000
Systran: http://www.systransoft.com
T 1 demo version: http://t1.sail-labs.com/t1probe.html

www.lim.nl/eamt

European association of Machine Translation

IAMT: international asc f MT

Glossary

32-bit application – A computer program that uses 32 bits to represent memory addresses. Windows 3.x, for example, is a 16-bit operating system, whereas the much faster Windows 95 and Windows NT are 32-bit operating systems.

Aligned texts – In translation-memory applications, the term 'aligned texts' refers to source and target texts or text fragments that have been determined as belonging together so that they can be reused by the translation memory system. The alignment process can be carried out manually by the user or automatically with the help of special software called an 'alignment tool'. The alignment process can be based on several strategies such as formatting information. The results can usually be modified and corrected by the user.

Ampersand – In software applications, the ampersand symbol (&) is used to indicate a *hotkey*.

ANSI – American National Standards Institute. An organization that creates standards for the computer industry. One of these standards is a text-only file format represented by the file extension *.ans.

Architecture – The basic structure or design of a computer or network system (including both hardware and software). The term 'client-server architecture', for example, indicates a system in which the basic components have specific roles and functions, in this case one computer that is offering data (*server*), and another that is requesting and receiving data (*client*).

Attribute – A specific characteristic of an object or term. In database and terminology management systems, 'attribute' is often synonymous with 'field'. In addition, MultiTerm uses 'attribute fields'. These contain classifying information such as the subject area that a term belongs to and etymological or grammatical information.

Archive – A file containing one or more compressed files.

ASCII – American Standard Code for Information Interchange. ASCII is a code for representing characters as numbers. Computers use ASCII codes to represent text. Like *ANSI* files, ASCII files are text-only; they do not contain any formatting information. This file format is represented by the file extension *.asc.

Basic rate interface – see *BRI*.

Bookmarking – Marking a specific document or database entry so that it can be retrieved more easily in the future. In WWW browsers, bookmarking features allow you to save the *URL* of a web document so you can revisit it faster in the future.

Boolean operators – Also called 'logical operators'. These operators, AND, OR and NOT, play an important role in *search engines* and are used to combine keywords in a number of ways. Combining two or more keywords using the AND operator tells the search engine to look for documents that contain all the keywords entered. The OR operator tells the search engine — or any retrieval software using these operators — to retrieve all documents containing any of the words. The NOT operator represents an exclusion command, meaning that you do not want to display any documents that contain the excluded word or words.

Bps – bits per second. The standard measure rate for the transmission of data.

BRI – Basic Rate Interface. One of two interfaces through which the *ISDN* service is provided to the end user. In Europe, BRI interfaces support two channels with a transmission rate of 64,000 bps each (56,000 bps in the United States).

Catalogue – A specific kind of Internet search utility, allowing the user to search for Internet resources by browsing though subject categories (e.g. Yahoo). Also referred to as a subject tree.

CAT – Computer-Assisted Translation. Any use of computers during the translation process.

CD-ROM – Compact Disc - Read-Only Memory. A mass storage device capable of storing large amounts of data (up to 680 Mb). CD-ROMs are often used as media for electronic dictionaries or encyclopedias.

Client – One component of a client-server *architecture*. An application running on a computer uses the capacities of a server to perform its tasks. An e-mail client, for example, is an application that enables you to send and receive e-mail.

Clipped text – In the *GUI* of a computer program (e.g. in a dialogue box), text that has been shortened in the translation process due to the fact that the number of characters available for the translated version was not sufficient.

Concordance – A set of examples of a given word or phrase showing the context of its occurrence in a corpus.

Configure – To set up a computer or an application.

Customize – The process of adapting a specific computer, program, corpus or text to the specific needs and interests of the user or reader (the customer).

DBMS – Database Management System. A type of application used for handling of vast amounts of structured data, e.g. terminology databases or client information.

Demo version – Versions of software programs distributed for promotional and testing purposes. Demo versions usually do not offer the application's complete list of features and/or are limited with regard to the duration of their usage.

Dialogue box – A display element used in *GUIs* to present information or to demand input from the user.

Digitization – The process of converting objects, e.g. texts or images, to digital form.

Distributed translation projects - Translation projects that are jointly being worked on by a group of geographically separated translators.

DVD – Digital Versatile Disc. A mass storage device capable of storing up to 4.7 Gb of data. Owing to their enormous storage capacities, DVDs have come to replace *CD-ROMs* and videotapes as a means of storing and playing multimedia applications and presentations.

EFT– Euro File Transfer. A *protocol* for the transmission of files over *ISDN* lines.

FAHQT – Fully Automatic High-Quality Translation; referring to *machine translation* systems capable of producing translations of a high quality, indistinguishable from those of human translators, without any form of human intervention.

File – A collection of data. There are different types of files, storing different types of data (e.g. text files, database files, program files). Files have filenames and file extensions, typically a three-letter code indicating the type of file (e.g. *.doc for a Word document).

Filter – A criterion for selecting data, e.g. terms in a database. Only data or terms matching the filter are allowed to pass, e.g. to be displayed on the screen or to be printed. For example, filtering the entries of a terminology database by using the subject field as a filter criterion (e.g. 'automotive') can allow the user to build a domain- specific glossary or a specialized dictionary.

FTP – File Transfer Protocol. An Internet service named after the *protocol* used to transfer files over the Internet. It allows you to access special computers called FTP servers, from which you can download files to your own computer or upload files to the FTP server. FTP is often used to transfer program updates. Some translation clients now deliver source texts and background information via FTP.

Fuzzy matching – Looking for terms in a terminology management system, or for phrases in a translation memory system, that are not identical with but show a certain similarity to the search criterion.

GTLD – Generic Top-Level Domain, also simply called 'top-level domains' (*TLDs*). Part of an Internet address (*URL*) used to help categorize Internet resources. GTLDs such as .com, .edu, or .org can be quite helpful for users who want to know what kind of institution they are about to access.

GUI – Graphical User Interface. A display format that allows the computer user to perform routine operations by selecting symbols or menus on the screen.

HAMT – Human-Assisted Machine Translation. A *CAT* scenario in which the computer does the translation of a text. The user's tasks are reduced to pre-editing and post-editing the source and target texts.

Hits – The number of occurrences of a keyword in a given collection of texts (e.g. in a corpus or on the Internet).

Hotkey – A key combination allowing the user to execute commands or change between applications by pressing a given sequence or combination of keys. Also referred to as a shortcut.

HTML – HyperText Markup Language. The authoring language in which most WWW documents are written.

HTTP – HyperText Transfer Protocol. The *protocol* upon which the transferring of WWW documents is based.

Hyperlink – An electronic reference linking one document to another document. By clicking on a hyperlink (a highlighted part of text), the document to which the link refers to is brought up on the screen. Hyperlinks are widely used on the WWW but also in online help files and in terminology management systems.

Hypermedia – An information system, e.g. an electronic dictionary or encyclopedia, that works like a *hypertext* system but which, in addition to text, also includes media such as graphics, video or sound.

Hypertext – A system of texts in which the single texts (objects) can be linked with one another by the use of electronic references called *hyperlinks*.

IRC – Internet Relay Chat. An Internet service named after the *protocol* on which it is based. It makes live online discussion between a large number of participants possible. The 'talking' (chatting) is done by typing your comments on the keyboard.

ISDN – Integrated Services Digital Network. A telecommunications network enabling the transmission of voice, data, audio and video over digital telephone lines.

One of its advantages is the high transmission rate of 64,000 bps. ISDN is delivered through two types of user interfaces: basic rate interface (*BRI*) and primary rate interface (*PRI*).

ISP – Internet Service Provider. A company providing access to the services of the Internet.

Kbps – Kilobits per second (1,000 bits per second). Measure rate for data transmission. See *Bps*.

L10N – See *localization*.

LAN – Local Area Network. A computer network that is confined to a relatively small area, e.g. an office building or a university campus.

Leverage – The recycling of identical or similar material. In translation memory systems, the re-use of pre-translated texts.

Localization – Often referred to as 'L10N'. The process of adapting a product to the specific situation of its target market. This includes not only translating the texts (and graphics) accompanying the product but also adapting it to the cultural norms of the local market.

Log file – A file listing a number of previously executed actions, e.g. previously visited websites or search items in a database.

MAHT – Machine-Assisted Human Translation. Any form of *CAT* in which the (human) translator translates the text but uses computer applications to support their work.

MIME – Multipurpose Internet Mail Extensions. A popular format for encoding files to be sent over the Internet.

MT – Machine Translation. The process of automatically translating any given source text using a computer program.

Parsing – The process of identifying a given character string as a sentence of a specific language.

PC – Personal Computer. A computer designed for use by only one person at a time.

Placeables – Variable elements in Trados' Translator's Workbench such as dates, numbers or measurements that should be adapted to the target language/culture during the localization process.

Pre-translation – In translation memory systems, the automatic translation of all segments from one or more documents that reach a certain match value (see fuzzy match) in the current translation memory prior to the actual translation of the source text.

PRI – Primary Rate Interface. One of two interfaces (see also *BRI*) through which the *ISDN* service is provided to the end user. In Europe, PRI interfaces support 30 channels with a transmission rate of 64,000 Bps each (23 channels with 56,000 Bps in the United States).

Primary Rate Interface – See *PRI*.

Protocol – A series of rules regulating the transfer of data over telephone lines or computer networks.

Propagating – In translation memory systems, the process of recycling duplicate material within the new text to be translated.

Provider – See *ISP*.

Raw translation – Euphemistically called 'informative translations'. The target-text output of *machine translation* systems with no human involvement.

Resizing tasks – Changing the size of *GUI* controls, e.g. menu titles or control buttons, to accommodate the length of the translated words.

Search engine – An Internet search utility that searches documents for keywords and returns a list of the Web documents where the keywords were found.

Server – A computer and/or software program that provides data resources over a computer network, e.g. the Internet or a *LAN*. Depending on the task of the server we can differentiate between a file server, a print server or a database server, among others.

Shortcut – See *hotkey*.

SimShip – The simultaneous international shipping of all target-market versions of a specific software product.

SMTP – Simple Mail Transfer Protocol. A protocol used by most e-mail systems to send e-mail messages between servers.

Subject tree – See *catalogue*.

TCP/IP – Transmission control protocol/Internet protocol. A series of protocols used to control the flow of data in large computer networks, such as the Internet.

TLD – Top-Level Domain. See *GTLD*.

TM – Terminology Management.

TMS – Translation Memory System.

Tracking – Keeping track of the files to be processed in a software-localization project.

URL – Uniform Resource Locator. The address of Internet resources.

WAIS – Wide Area Information Service. A primitive search program for finding documents on the Internet.

Wildcard – Also called 'wildcard character'. A special symbol, e.g. * or ?, that stands for one or more characters.

WYSIWYG – What You See Is What You Get. The ability of software, e.g. a desktop publishing application or a Web editor, to display a document on the screen in exactly the same way as it will appear when the document is printed or published on the Internet.

Zipping – A method for compressing (i.e. reducing the size of) files. Named after a popular compression format (see also *archive*).

References

Ackermann, E. & K. Hartman (1998) *The Information Specialist's Guide to Searching and Researching on the Internet and the World Wide Web*, Wilsonville, OR: Abf Content.

Albrecht, J., F. Austermühl and J. Kornelius (eds) (1998) *etb – electronic term books*, Trier: WVT Wissenschaftlicher.

Alwang, G. (1998) *Better Translation. Need to Communicate across Borders? Globalink's new program helps you remove language barriers*, PC Magazine, December 14, http://www.zdnet.com/products/stories/reviews/0,4161,373377,00.html. (1 March 2001)

Arnold, D., L. Balken, L. Humphreys, S. Meijer and L. Sadler (eds) (1994) *Machine Translation. An Introductory Guide*, London: NCC Blackwell.

Arntz, R. and H. Picht (1989) *Einführung in die Terminologiearbeit*, Hildesheim, Zürich, New York: Olms.

ASSIM (1997) *Interim Report: Assessment of the Economic and Social Impact of Multilingualism in Europe*, http://www.hltcentral.org/usr_docs/project-source/Assim/Assim-EN.doc. (1 March 2001)

Austermühl, F. (1999) 'Between Babel and Bytes – The Discipline of Translation in the Information Age', in *AREAS – Annual Report on English and American Studies* 16, Trier: WVT Wissenschaftlicher, 439-450.

------ (forthcoming) *Übersetzen im Informationszeitalter - Überlegungen zur Zukunft fachkommunikativen und interkulturellen Handelns im Global Village*, Trier: WVT Wissenschaftlicher.

Austermühl, F. and J. Kornelius (1993) 'Über die Verfügbarkeit elektronischer Hilfsmittel in Übersetzungsdiensten: Die Ergebnisse einer Befragung', in *Anglistik & Englischunterricht* 51, Heidelberg: Universitätsverlag C. Winter, 175-190.

------ (1995) 'Sprachdatenbanken und Terminologieverwaltungssysteme in der Übersetzungspraxis', in *Anglistik & Englischunterricht* 55/56, Heidelberg: Universitätsverlag C. Winter, 197-220.

Austermühl, F. and M. Coners (forthcoming) *Computer-assisted Terminology Management*, Translation Practices Explained series, Manchester: St. Jerome.

Austermühl, F., E. Einhauser and J. Kornelius (1998) 'Die elektronischen Hilfsmittel des Übersetzers', in AREAS *Annual Report on English and American Studies* 16, Trier: WVT Wissenschaftlicher, 335-381.

Baker, M. (1996) 'Corpus-based Translation Studies: The Challenges that Lie Ahead', in Harold Somers (ed) *Terminology, LSP and Translation: Studies in Language Engineering in Honour of Juan C. Sager*, Amsterdam & Philadelphia: Benjamins, 175-186.

------ (1999) 'The Role of Corpora in Investigating the Linguistic Behaviour of Professional Translators', in *International Journal of Corpus Linguistics* 4(2), 281-298.

Beck, U. (1998) *Was ist Globalisierung?*, Frankfurt am Main: Suhrkamp, 5th edition.

Berners-Lee, T., M. Fischetti and M. Dertouzos (1999) *Weaving the Web: The Original Design and Ultimate Destiny of the World Wide Web by its Inventor*, San Francisco: Harper.

Blatt, A., K.-H. Freigang, K.-D. Schmitz and G. Thome (eds) (1985) *Computer und Übersetzen*, Hildesheim, Zürich, New York: Georg Olms.

Brace, C., M. Vasconcellos and C. Miller (1995) *MT Users and Usage: Europe and the Americas*, http://www.lim.nl/eamt/archive/summit95.html. (1 March 2001)

Bradley, Stephen P., Richard L. Nolan and Jerry A. Hausman (eds) (1993) *Globalization, Technology, and Competition: the fusion of computers and telecommunications in the 1990s*, Boston, Mass.: Harvard Business School Press.

Brown, G. and G. Yule (1983) *Discourse Analysis*, Cambridge: Cambridge University Press.

Brungs, B. (1996) *Translation Memories als Komponente Integrierter Übersetzungssysteme*, Saarbrücker Studien zur Sprachdatenverarbeitung und Übersetzen, Band 7, Saarbrücken: Fachbereich 8.6 – Angewandte Sprachwissenschaft sowie Übersetzen und Dolmetschen, Universität des Saarlands.

Chiu A. L. S., E. Sherry and X. Phung (1999) 'Just try to be specific', in *Nature* 401/6749, 111.

Cohen, J. and J. Ward (1998) 'World's wide Web needs to speak its languages', *CNN interactive*, http://www.cnn.com/TECH/computing/9810/26/lang.idg. (1 March 2001)

Cole, R.A., J. Mariani, J. Uszkoreit, A. Zaenen and V. Zue (1996) *Survey of the State of the Art in Human Language Technology*, http://cslu.cse.ogi.edu/HLTsurvey/. (1 March 2001)

Der Spiegel (1996) 'Klick in die Zukunft', in *Der Spiegel* 11/96, 66-99.

Dohler, P. (1996) 'Facets of Software Localization', in *Language Partners International*, http://www.languagepartners.com/reference-center/whitepapers/l10nwp/triacom.htm. (1 March 2001)

Dyson, E. (1998) *Release 2.1: A Design for Living in the Digital Age*, New York: Broadway Books.

Esselink, B. (1998) *A Practical Guide to Software Localization*, Amsterdam &, Philadelphia: John Benjamins.

European Commission (1999) *A Multilingual Community at Work. The European Commission's Translation Service*, Luxembourg: Office for Official Publications of the European Communities. http://europa.eu.int/comm/translation/en/enintro.html. (1 March 2001)

Feldmann, Doris, Fritz-Wilhelm Neumann and Thomas Rommel (eds) (1997) *Anglistik im Internet – Proceedings of the 1996 Erfurt Conference on Computing in the Humanities*, Heidelberg: Universitätsverlag C. Winter.

Gantz, J. (1998) 'Coming soon: Language barriers', in *Computerworld*, 2 Feb. 1998. http://www.computerworld.com/cwi/story/0,1199,NAV47_STO13396,00.html. (1 March 2001)

Gralla, Preston (ed), Sarah Ishida, Mina Reimer and Stephen Adams (illustrators) (1999) *How the Internet Works: Millennium Edition*, Indianapolis: Que.

Gross, A. (1992) 'Limitations of Computers as Translation Tools', in J. Newton (ed) *Computers in Translation*, London: Routledge, 96-130.

Gurian, Phil (1996) *E-mail Business Strategies*, Spokane: Grand National Press.

Harris, R. (1997) 'Evaluating Internet Research Sources', http://www.sccu.edu/faculty/R_Harris/evalu8it.htm. (1 March 2001)

Hausmann, F. J., O. Reichmann, H. E. Wiegand and L. Zgusta (eds) (1989) *Wörterbücher – Dictionaries – Dictionnaires. Ein internationales Handbuch zur Lexikographie*, Handbücher zur Sprach- und Kommunikationswissenschaft, vol. 5.1, Berlin & New York: De Gruyter.

Heynold, C. (1996) 'Die EU und ihre Sprachen. Elfmal verbindlich', in *EUMagazin* 12, 50-54.

Hock, R. and P. Berinstein (1999) *The Extreme Searcher's Guide to Web Search Engines: A Handbook for the Serious Searcher*, Medford, N.J.: Information Today Inc.

Holderbaum, A. (1999) 'Kriterien der Evaluation elektronischer Wörterbücher – am Beispiel der CD-ROM-Version des Oxford Advanced Learner's Dictionary of Current English', in *AREAS – Annual Report on English and American Studies* 17, Trier: WVT Wissenschaftlicher, 365-386.

Holmes, J.S. (1988) *Translated! – Papers on Literary Translation and Translation Studies*, Amsterdam: Rodopi.

Hönig, Hans G. (1998) 'Textverstehen und Recherchieren', in Mary Snell-Hornby, Hans G. Hönig, Paul Kußmaul and Peter A. Schmitt (eds) *Handbuch Translation*, Tübingen: Stauffenburg, 160-164.

Hughes, Lawrence E. (1998) *Internet E-mail: Protocols, Standards, and Implementation* (Artech House Telecommunications Library), Norwood: Artech House.

Huntington, S. (1996) *The Clash of Civilizations and the Remaking of World Order*, New York: Simon & Schuster.

Hupka, W. (1989) 'Das enzyklopädische Wörterbuch', in F. J. Hausmann, O. Reichmann, H. E. Wiegang and L. Zgusta (eds) *Wörterbücher – Dictionaries – Dictionnaires. Ein internationales Handbuch zur Lexikographie* (Handbücher zur Sprach- und Kommunikationswissenschaft, vol. 5.1), Berlin & New York: De Gruyter, 988-999.

Hutchins, J. (1996) *Computer-based Translation Systems and Tools*, http://www.lim.nl/ eamt/archive/hutchins_intro.html. (1 March 2001)

Hutchins, J. & H. Somers (1992) *An Introduction to Machine Translation*, London: Academic Press Ltd.

Kay, M. (1996) 'Machine Translation: The Disappointing Past and Present', in Cole, R.A., J. Mariani, J. Uszkoreit, A. Zaenen and V. Zue (1996) *Survey of the State of the Art in Human Language Technology*, http://cslu.cse.ogi.edu/HLTsurvey/ch8node4.html#SECTION82/. (1 March 2001)

Kehoe, B. P. (1992) *Zen and the Art of the Internet. A Beginner's Guide to the Internet*, First Edition, January 1992, http://www.cs.indiana.edu/docproject/zen/zen-1.0_toc.html. (1 March 2001)

Lehrberger, J. and L. Bourbeau (1998) *Machine Translation: Linguistic characteristics of MT systems and general methodology of evaluation*, Amsterdam & Philadelphia: John Benjamins.

Lernout&Hauspie (1998) *Lernout&Hauspie Power Translator receives A Peak Performance Award At SpeechTek 98*, http://www.lhs.com/news/releases/19981109_PTAward.asp. (1 March 2001)

------ (2000) *Preparing English Source Text*, http://www.lhsl.com/uk/powertranslator/text_eng.asp. (1 March 2001)

Lockwood, R. (1998) 'Global English and Language Market Trends', in *Language International* 10/4, 16-18.

------ (2000) 'Machine Translation and Controlled Authoring at Caterpillar', in R. Sprung (ed) *Translating Into Success. Cutting-edge strategies for going multilingual in a global age*, American Translators Association Scholarly Monograph Series, Volume XI, Amsterdam & Philadelphia: John Benjamins, 187-202.

Lockwood, R., J. Leston and L. Lachal (1995) *Globalisation – Creating New Markets with Translation Technology*, London: Ovum Limited.

Mai, J. and S. Wettach (1999) 'Verbales Rüstzeug', in *WirtschaftsWoche* 21, 130-138.

Malone, T. W. and J. R. Rockart (1993) 'How Will Information Technology Reshape Organizations? Computers as Coordination Technology', in Stephen P. Bradley, Richard L. Nolan and Jerry A. Hausman (eds) *Globalization, Technology, and Competition: the fusion of computers and telecommunications in the 1990s*, Boston, Mass.: Harvard Business School Press, 37-56.

Markl, H. (1998) *Wissenschaft gegen Zukunftsangst*, Wien, München: Carl Hanser Verlag.

McEnery, T. and A. Wilson (1996) *Corpus Linguistics*, Edinburgh: Edinburgh University Press.

McLuhan, M. (1967) *The Gutenberg Galaxy*, London: Routledge & Kegan Paul.

McLuhan, M. and B. R. Powers (1989) *The Global Village: Transformations in World Life and Media in the 21st Century*, New York: Oxford University Press.

Melby, A. K. (1982) 'Multi-level translation aids in a distributed system', in J. Horecký (ed) *Proceedings of COLING 82*, Amsterdam: North Holland Publishing Company, 215-220.

------ (1992) 'The translator workstation', in J. Newton (ed) *Computers in Translation*, London: Routledge, 147-165.

------ (1995) *The Possibility of Language*, Amsterdam & Philadelphia: John Benjamins.

------ (1998) *Eight Types of Translation Technology*. http://www.ttt.org/technology/8types.pdf. (1 March 2001)

Miller, S. (1998) *Searching the World Wide Web – An Introductory Curriculum for Using Search Engines*, Eugene, OR: International Society for Technology in Education.

Neumann, F.-W. (1997) 'Geisteswissenschaften im Internet – Möglichkeiten und Grenzen einer Technologie', in D. Feldmann et al. *Anglistik im Internet – Proceedings of the 1996 Erfurt Conference on Computing in the Humanities*, Heidelberg: Universitätsverlag C. Winter, 47-72.

Nord, Christiane (1997) *Translating as a Purposeful Activity. Functionalist Approaches Explained*, Manchester: St. Jerome.

O'Hagan, M. (1996) *The Coming Industry of Teletranslation: Overcoming Communication Barriers Through Telecommunication*, Clevedon: Multilingual Matters.

Ouedet, B. (1998) 'Multilingualism on the Internet. UNESCO's Observatory on the Information Society'. http://www.unesco.org/webworld/observatory/themes/multilingual /diversity/doc_sp_1.html. (1 March 2001)

Papows, J. (1998) *Enterprise.com – Market Leadership in the Information Age*, Reading, Mass.: Perseus Books.

Pearson, J. (1998) *Terms in Context*, Amsterdam & Philadelphia: John Benjamins.

Pym, A. (1998) 'Ausbildungssituation in aller Welt (Überblick)', in Mary Snell-Hornby, Hans G. Hönig, Paul Kußmaul and Peter A. Schmitt. (eds) *Handbuch Translation*, Tübingen: Stauffenburg, 33-36.

Raeithel, G. (1999) 'Brodeln im Sprachmeer', in *Süddeutsche Zeitung* 10/11 July 1999, I.

Rey, A. (1995) *Essays on Terminology Processing*, Amsterdam & Philadelphia: John Benjamins.

Rudolph, Mark T. (1998) *Correo electrónico qué fácil*, Barcelona: Marcombo.

Schäler, R. (1996) 'Machine Translation, Translation Memories and the Phrasal Lexicon: The Localisation Perspective', in *Proceedings of the EAMT Workshop*, TKE 96, Vienna, Austria, 29-30 August 1996, 21-34. http://www.lim.nl/eamt/archive/vienna.pdf. (1 March 2001).

Schmidt, P. (1998) 'Automatisches Übersetzen', in Mary Snell-Hornby, Hans G. Hönig, Paul Kußmaul and Peter A. Schmitt (eds) *Handbuch Translation*, Tübingen: Stauffenburg, 133-137.

Schmitt, P. A. (1998) 'Technische Arbeitsmittel', in Mary Snell-Hornby, Hans G. Hönig, Paul Kußmaul and Peter A. Schmitt (eds) *Handbuch Translation*, Tübingen: Stauffenburg, 186-199.

Schneider, T. (1991) 'Ohne Sprache keine Chance', in Siemens Nixdorf Informationssysteme (ed) *Dialog Special, Informations-Automatisierung*, 1/91, Ausgabe März.

Schwanke, M. (1991) *Maschinelle Übersetzung. Ein Überblick über Theorie und Praxis*, Berlin & Heidelberg: Springer Verlag.

Siemens Nixdorf Informationssysteme AG (1997) *HighPrint 4905/4905L – Bedienungsanleitung*, Munich: Siemens Nixdorf Informationssysteme AG.

Sikló, Marie (forthcoming) *Localization Explained*, Manchester: St Jerome.

Smith, N., T. McEnery and R. Ivanic (1998) 'Issues in transcribing a corpus of children's handwritten projects', in *Literary and Linguistic Computing* 13/4, 217-226.

Snell-Hornby, M., H. G. Hönig, P. Kußmaul and P. A. Schmitt (eds) (1998) *Handbuch Translation*, Tübingen: Stauffenburg.

Snell-Hornby, M. (1998) 'Ausbildungssituation in Europa', in Mary Snell-Hornby, Hans G. Hönig, Paul Kußmaul and Peter A. Schmitt (eds) *Handbuch Translation*, Tübingen: Stauffenburg, 31-33

Spies, C. (1995) *Vergleichende Untersuchung von integrierten Übersetzungssystemen mit Translation-memory-Komponente*, Saarbrücker Studien zu Sprachdatenverarbeitung und Übersetzen, Band 3, Saarbrücken: Fachbereich 8.6 – Angewandte Sprachwissenschaft sowie Übersetzen und Dolmetschen, Universität des Saarlands.

Sprung, R. C. (ed) (2000) *Translating Into Success. Cutting-edge strategies for going multilingual in a global age*, American Translators Association Scholarly Monograph Series, Volume XI, Amsterdam & Philadelphia: John Benjamins.

Stoll, K. (1999) 'Interkulturelle Anglophonie', in *Lebende Sprachen* 1/99, 14-20.

Tunstall, Joan (1996) *Better, Faster Email: Getting the Most Out of Email*, St.

Leonards: Allen & Unwin.

Tuthill, B. and D. Smallberg (1997) *Creating Worldwide Software: Solaris International Developer's Guide*, Upper Saddle River: Prentice Hall, 2nd edition.

Vasconcellos, M. (1999) *Users of Systems. The Current State of MT Usage. Or: How do I Use Thee? Let Me Count the Ways.* http://www.lim.nl/eamt/archive/summit93.html. (1 March 2001)

Vermeer, H.J. (1986) 'Übersetzen als kultureller Transfer', in Mary Snell-Hornby (ed) *Übersetzungswissenschaft – eine Neuorientierung. Zur Integrierung von Theorie und Praxis*, Tübingen: Francke, 30-53.

Webb, L. (1998) *Advantages and Disadvantages of Translation Memory – A Cost / Benefit Analysis.* http://www.webbsnet.com/translation/thesis.html. (1 March 2001)

Weber, N. (1998) 'Machine Translation, Evaluation, and Translation Quality Assessment', in N. Weber (ed) *Machine Translation: Theory, Applications, and Evaluation. An assessment of the state-of-the-art*, St. Augustin: Gardez! Verlag, 47-84.

Wilss, W. (1988) *Kognition und Übersetzen. Zu Theorie und Praxis der menschlichen und maschinellen Übersetzung*, Tübingen: Max Niemeyer Verlag.

Winchester, S. (1998) *The Professor and the Madman: A Tale of Murder, Insanity, and the Making of the Oxford English Dictionary*, New York: HarperCollins.

Wood, J. (1998) 'Career building', *Language International* 10/4, 12-15, 47.

Wright, S. E. and G. Budin (1997) *Handbook of Terminology Management. Vol. 1: Basic aspects of Terminology Management*, Amsterdam & Philadelphia: John Benjamins.

------ (forthcoming) *Handbook of Terminology Management. Vol. 1I*, Amsterdam & Philadelphia: John Benjamins.

Index

Translation Practices Explained

Series titles